HERESIES AND HOW TO AVOID THEM

Why it matters what Christians believe

Edited by
Ben Quash and Michael Ward

Foreword by Stanley Hauerwas

BakerAcademic
a division of Baker Publishing Group
Grand Rapids, Michigan

© 2007 by Ben Quash and Michael Ward
Individual chapters © the contributors 2007

Published by Baker Academic
a division of Baker Publishing Group
P.O. Box 6287, Grand Rapids, MI 49516-6287
www.bakeracademic.com

Baker Academic edition published 2012
ISBN 978-0-8010-4749-7

Previously published in 2007 by Hendrickson Publishers in the United States and SPCK
in Great Britain
Hendrickson ISBN 978-1-59856-013-8
SPCK ISBN 978-0-281-05843-3

Printed in the United States of America

Library of Congress Cataloging-in-Publication Data for the original edition is on file at
the Library of Congress, Washington, DC.

The internet addresses, email addresses, and phone numbers in this book are accurate at
the time of publication. They are provided as a resource. Baker Publishing Group does
not endorse them or vouch for their content or permanence.

15   16   17   18   7   6   5   4   3

Contents

Part 1
HERESIES OF THE PERSON OF CHRIST
AND HOW TO AVOID THEM

Contents

Part 2
HERESIES OF THE CHURCH AND CHRISTIAN LIVING
AND HOW TO AVOID THEM

Notes on contributors

Dr Nicholas Adams, an Anglican, is Lecturer in Systematic Theology and Theological Ethics at the University of Edinburgh. He has a doctorate in theology from the University of Cambridge, where he also pursued post-doctoral study on Jürgen Habermas's account of religion while a Research Fellow at Trinity Hall. His publications include *Habermas and Theology* (Cambridge University Press, 2006) and a number of articles which consider the relationship between German philosophy in the nineteenth century and Christian theology in the twentieth.

The Revd Dr Anders Bergquist, an Anglican priest, is Vicar of St John's Wood in central London. He has a doctorate in archaeology from the University of Cambridge and taught Early Christian Life and Thought in the Cambridge Theological Federation (1989–97), where he was Vice-Principal of Westcott House (1995–97). He was responsible for continuing ministerial education in the Diocese of St Albans (1997–2002) and is the co-editor of *Biblical Interpretation in the Early Church: An Historical Introduction to Patristic Exegesis* (T&T Clark, 1994).

Dr Janet Martin Soskice, a Roman Catholic, is a Fellow of Jesus College and Reader in Modern Theology and Philosophical Theology in the University of Cambridge. She has a doctorate in the philosophy of religion from the University of Oxford and is the author of *Metaphor and Religious Language* (Clarendon Press, 1985), the editor of *After Eve* (Marshall Pickering, 1990), and the co-editor of *Medicine and Moral Reasoning* (Cambridge University Press, 1994) and *Feminism and Theology* (Oxford University Press, 2003).

Dr Rachel Muers, a member of the Religious Society of Friends (Quakers), is a Lecturer in Theology at the University of Exeter. She has a doctorate in theology from the University of Cambridge, where she held a Research Fellowship at Girton College. Her publications include *Keeping God's Silence: Towards a Theological Ethics of Communication* (Blackwell, 2004).

Dr Marcus Plested, a member of the Eastern Orthodox Church, is Vice-Principal of the Institute for Orthodox Christian Studies in the Cambridge Theological Federation and Research Associate in the Faculty of Divinity of the University of Cambridge. He has a doctorate in theology from the University of Oxford, and his most recent book is *The Macarian Legacy: The Place of Macarius-Symeon in the Eastern Christian Tradition* (Oxford University Press, 2004).

The Revd Canon Professor Ben Quash, an Anglican priest, is Professor of Christianity and the Arts at King's College, London, and Canon Theologian of Coventry Cathedral. He has a doctorate in theology from the University of Cambridge, and his publications include *Theology and the Drama of History* (Cambridge University Press, 2005) and *Fields of Faith: Theology and Religious Studies for the 21st Century* (Cambridge University Press, 2005), edited with David F. Ford and Janet Martin Soskice.

The Revd Canon John Sweet, an Anglican priest, is a Fellow of Selwyn College in the University of Cambridge, where he was Chaplain, then Dean of Chapel (1958–94). He was a Lecturer in New Testament in the Cambridge Divinity Faculty (1960–94) and holds a Lambeth Doctorate in Divinity. His publications include *Revelation* (SCM Press, 1979) and *Early Christian Thought in its Jewish Context*, edited with John Barclay (Cambridge University Press, 1996).

The Revd Dr Michael B. Thompson, an Anglican priest, is Vice-Principal of Ridley Hall and Lecturer in Greek and the

New Testament in the Cambridge Theological Federation. He has a doctorate in theology from the University of Cambridge, which was published as *Clothed with Christ* (JSOT Press, 1992). He co-edited *A Vision for the Church: Studies in Early Christian Ecclesiology* (T&T Clark, 1997), and his other books include *Transforming Grace* (Bible Reading Fellowship, 1998) and *When Should We Divide?* (Grove Books, 2004).

The Revd Angela Tilby, an Anglican priest, is Vicar of St Benet's, Cambridge, and Lecturer in Early Church History and Spirituality in the Cambridge Theological Federation. She read theology at Girton College in the University of Cambridge and then worked for the British Broadcasting Corporation as a radio and television producer (1973–97). She was Vice-Principal of Westcott House (2001–06), and her publications include *Let There Be Light: Praying with Genesis* (Darton, Longman & Todd, 2006), *God Before Breakfast* (SPCK, 2005), and *Son of God* (Hodder & Stoughton, 2001).

Professor Denys Turner, a Roman Catholic, is Horace Tracy Pitkin Professor of Historical Theology at the University of Yale. Formerly Norris-Hulse Professor of Divinity at the University of Cambridge and H. G. Wood Professor of Theology at the University of Birmingham, he is the author of several monographs on medieval mystical theology, including *Faith, Reason and the Existence of God* (Cambridge University Press, 2004), *The Darkness of God* (Cambridge University Press, 1995), and *Eros and Allegory* (Cistercian Publications, 1995). He has also published a collection of sermons and talks under the title of *Faith Seeking* (SCM Press, 2002).

The Revd Dr Michael Ward, an Anglican priest, is a writer. He was Chaplain of Peterhouse in the University of Cambridge and Assistant Curate at St Mary's, Great Shelford (2004–2007). He has a doctorate in theology from the University of St Andrews and his publications include *Planet Narnia: The Seven Heavens in the Imagination of C. S. Lewis* (Oxford University Press, 2007;

<www.planetnarnia.com>) and the forthcoming *Cambridge Companion to C. S. Lewis.*

Dr Anna Williams (A. N. Williams), an Anglican, is a Fellow of Corpus Christi College and Lecturer in Patristic and Medieval Theology in the University of Cambridge. She has a doctorate in theology from the University of Yale, where she occupied the chair in Anglican Studies. Her publications include *The Divine Sense: The Intellect in Patristic Theology* (Cambridge University Press, 2006) and *The Ground of Union: Deification in Aquinas and Palamas* (Oxford University Press, 1999).

Foreword

PROFESSOR STANLEY HAUERWAS

————◦◦◦————

In a time when the Church seems more confused than faithful, some may wonder whether a book that reprises discussions of ancient heresies is needed. Given the diminished state of the Church some Christians might even believe that if we could gain more members by being heretical so much the worse for orthodoxy. That is why this book is so important – because the following chapters (most of which began life as sermons) rightly help us see that how we speak as Christians makes all the difference if we are to be faithful witnesses in a confused Church and in an even more confused world.

It is extremely important to note that this book originated in a sermon series. For the testing of Christian speech is prayer. The decisive form of prayer is the liturgy in which the sermon is one of the central acts of praise. The Church's doctrinal debates are rightly about how we are to pray so that our words do not betray the one to whom we pray. Situating the discussion of past heresies within the liturgical action of the Church and, in particular, its proclamation, indicates the continuing need of the Church to speak well in the appropriate context.

Moreover, that the heresies are dissected through sermons reminds us that theology is always first and foremost commentary on Scripture. Each of these essays in distinct ways shows how Christian reading of the Bible is a delicate task at once as beautiful and complex as a spider's web. Spiderwebs are fragile, requiring constant repair, which means the web in the process of repair reveals connections we had not anticipated. If there is, as these chapters suggest, an order to heresies, it is also true that there is an order to orthodoxy. That order is at once beautiful and fragile – beautiful because of its fragility.

That one of the tests of orthodoxy is beauty means orthodoxy betrays itself if it is used as a hammer to beat into submission those we think heterodox (not conforming with orthodox belief). Thus it is significant that the following chapters do not demonize the heretics of the past and present. The Church seldom knows what it believes until someone gets it wrong. Indeed, often it is not even clear at the beginning what has been got wrong. So those who get it wrong are blessed just to the extent that they help us discover what it is we must faithfully say, to be adequate witnesses to God.

Orthodoxy can tempt us to self-righteousness and a protectiveness that betrays the joy and confidence that should be the heart of the gospel. When orthodoxy becomes defensive rather than a form of love and proclamation it denies its own reality. These essays rightly demonstrate the lively and radical character of orthodoxy which does not require coercion to sustain itself. Rather orthodoxy is displayed as an act of love that takes the form of careful speech.

When all is said and done orthodoxy is the hard discipline of learning to say what needs to be said and no more. Too often those we learn to call heretics have tried to say more than can be said. They have succumbed to the temptation to say too much by explaining what cannot be explained. Orthodoxy shows why what we believe cannot be explained but can only be prayed. What Christians believe is wonderfully simple, but to say what is simple is not easy. That, again, is why it is so important that these exemplifications of orthodoxy initially took the form of sermons, so that we might rightly locate what needs to be said in the very life of the Church.

Let us hope this book will be for many an introduction to the Christian faith that is as informative as it is attractive and interesting. I am not surprised that many hearing these sermons wished to have them in print. For there is a lightness of touch, a profound sense of humour, and a liveliness to the following pages that cannot help but attract Christians and non-Christians alike who might want to know better what it is the Church has discovered we believe. I hope this book will serve to remind us that, as confusing as our current ecclesial situation may seem, there are indeed signs of hope as Christians rediscover the beauty of the language necessary to praise the God who has gifted us through the Spirit of his Son.

To William and Joseph Quash
and
to Keith and Olive Ward

Prologue

BEN QUASH

Ideas achieve the status of heresies in Christian tradition because they are thought by the Church to be wrong rather than right teaching, or 'doctrine'. A heretic is a baptized person who obstinately denies or doubts a truth which the Church teaches must be believed because it is part of the one, divinely revealed, and catholic (that is, universally valid) Christian faith.

To our modern liberal ears an interest in the rights and wrongs of doctrine may sound a bit of a pedantic interest to have – and even a recipe for intolerance and persecution. We tend to think that people's beliefs, and especially their religious beliefs, are their own business, and should be respected as such. But there is a very good and positive reason why Christianity has been so concerned about orthodoxy, or right belief. From its very beginnings, Christianity said that neither your race, nor your sex, nor your social class, nor your age could ever be a bar to full membership of Christ's body, the Church. Anyone could be a Christian: you didn't have to be born in the right place at the right time to the right parents. Christ's salvation was offered to you whether or not you were a Jew or a Gentile, a slave or free person, a woman or a man. This was radical stuff. What, though, was left to mark a Christian out from a non-Christian? The answer was: your faith – what you believed in, as embodied in your practices and confessed with your lips. The Church's identity and integrity were expressed in orthodoxy: the confession (and enactment) of a collective belief. Christianity was open to anyone, but it had definite convictions. That's why heresy was a matter to be taken seriously, because it called those

1

convictions into question. It threatened a crucial thing that bound the Church together and made Christians Christians.

Irenaeus of Lyons (*c.* 130–*c.* 200) was perhaps the first really great *catholic* theologian of the Church (both East and West) – and his massive principal work recognized exactly this point, namely, that from a Christian point of view heresies are not to be taken lightly, and can be positively dangerous to the community of faith. His great work, *Against Heresies*, was devoted to a vigorous and detailed engagement with all that threatened the delicate and saving coherence of Christian truth. It asserts the power of that truth to liberate the believer from error and the self-serving projection of things we *want* to be true (perhaps because they suit us better, confirm our pre-judices, or are somehow easier to accommodate).

The language of attack he uses is vigorous, but there is a curious recognition in what he says that the heretics' real menace is not their out-and-out hostility to the convictions and teachings of the true Church, but the insidious way they assimilate themselves to Christian orthodoxy. Heretics, for example, frequently make use of Scripture – drawing on the same sources as the orthodox in most cases. This is a big part of the problem: what they produce looks so plausible, so legitimate:

> They endeavour to adapt with an air of probability to their own peculiar assertions the parables of the Lord, the sayings of the prophets, and the words of the apostles, in order that their scheme may not seem altogether without support. (*Against Heresies*, Book I, Chapter 8, paragraph 1)

In the chapters that follow, you will see how time and again scriptural interpretation is at the core of disputes between positions that would eventually be declared orthodox and those that would eventually be declared heretical. Though Irenaeus is not inclined to generosity on this matter – too much, for him, was at stake – it emerges that in many cases the heretics-to-be were positively anxious to be true to Scripture; they were scrupulous in their use of it. The citation of passages from Scripture at the beginning of each chapter in the present book acknowledges this fact – so that sometimes the passages illustrate key texts appealed to by the orthodox to refute the 'peculiar assertions' (as Irenaeus would put it) of the heretics, but sometimes they are there because they were adopted as key platforms for heretical argument.

One thing this should probably teach us is that 'proof-texting' (citation of fragments of the Bible out of context) is never enough in the application of Scripture to Christian doctrinal issues. But there is a further lesson to be learned from the history of heresy – not unrelated – which is that individual doctrinal issues themselves cannot be considered in a stand-alone way. Exclusive and narrow focus on one issue can take one's eye off another, and begin to have distorting effects on it. There is no better illustration of this than the tight integrity of the historic responses to the first four heresies treated in this book (all of them concerned with the person of Jesus Christ). Anna Williams shows helpfully in the opening paragraphs of her chapter how there is 'an order to heresies' – and to these in particular. Each doctrinal affirmation in the series of four needs the others to balance, correct and contextualize it, and together – as was also recognized by the great Anglican theologian Richard Hooker (*c.* 1554–1600) – they are exquisitely poised. Take one away, and the others are rendered more prone to misinterpretation – and the recurrence of old heresies in new forms at later points in history demonstrates how the mind of the Church needs to be kept alert to all of them. Hooker writes:

> There are but four things which concur to make complete the whole state of our Lord Jesus Christ: his Deity, his manhood, the conjunction of both, and the distinction of the one from the other being joined in one. Four principal heresies there are which have in those things withstood the truth: Arians by

bending themselves against the Deity of Christ; Apollinarians [Docetists] by maiming and misinterpreting that which belongeth to his human nature; Nestorians by rending Christ asunder, and dividing him into two persons; the followers of Eutyches by confounding in his person those natures which they should distinguish. Against these there have been four most famous ancient general councils: the council of Nicea to define against Arians, against Apollinarians the council of Constantinople, the council of Ephesus against Nestorians, against Eutychians the Chalcedon council. In four words ... *truly, perfectly, indivisibly, distinctly*, the first applied to His being God [versus Arianism], and the second to His being Man [versus Apollinarianism], the third to His being of both One [versus Nestorianism], and the fourth to His still continuing that one Both [versus Eutychianism], we may fully by way of abridgment comprise whatsoever antiquity hath at large handled either in declaration of Christian belief, or in refutation of the foresaid heresies. Within the compass of which four heads, I may truly affirm, that all heresies which touch but the person of Jesus Christ, whether they have risen in these later days, or in any age heretofore, may be with great facility brought to confine themselves. (Richard Hooker, *The Laws of Ecclesiastical Polity*, Book V, Chapter 54, paragraph 10)

There is an order to heresies, and a coherence in the rules that were developed for helping us to avoid them. The structure of this book is partly lent to it by that order which is in the heresies and that coherence which is in the reactions. A series of moves and countermoves in relation to understanding the person of Jesus Christ generated the Church's grammar of orthodoxy in its Christology or doctrine of Christ (Chapters 1 to 4) and, indeed, in its doctrine of the Trinity (the belief that God is three persons, Father, Son and Holy Spirit, in one substance). The Church was then equipped to respond decisively to the aftershocks of earlier Christological controversies that continued to be registered in heresies like Adoptionism and Theopaschitism (Chapters 5 and 6). These heresies and the responses they provoked make sense as a group. And if they have in common a focus on what is *saving* about Jesus Christ (among other things), the second group of heresies are responses to the question: 'What must *we do* to be saved?' These (Chapters 7 to 11) circle, often overlappingly, around the desire to refine, purify, even rarefy Christian Scripture, tradition, knowledge and practice. Here too there are identifiable strands of concern that relate the heresies and reveal consistency in the orthodoxy they offend.

The key task for orthodoxy, it seems, is to keep a sense of what the larger shape of Christian belief is – a shape which, if contemplated patiently and sensitively and with a concern to find its maximum integrity, will unlock its inner persuasive power, and display its glory. Irenaeus uses the memorable image of a mosaic to fix in the minds of his readers this concern with the integrity of the 'whole picture'. He says of the heretics that in seeking the 'air of probability' that they so desire for their assertions they disregard 'order and . . . connection':

Their manner of acting is just as if one, when a beautiful image of a king has been constructed by some skilful artist out of precious jewels, should then take this likeness of the man all to pieces, should rearrange the gems, and so fit them together as to make them into the form of a dog or of a fox, and even that but poorly executed; and should then maintain and declare that *this* was the beautiful image of the king which the skilful artist constructed, pointing to the jewels which had been admirably fitted together by the first artist to form the image of the king, but have been with bad effect transferred by the latter one to the shape of a dog, and by thus exhibiting the jewels, should deceive the ignorant who had no conception what a king's form was like, and persuade them that that miserable likeness of the fox was, in fact, the beautiful image of the king. In like manner do these persons patch together old wives' fables, and then endeavour, by violently drawing away from their proper connection, words, expressions, and parables whenever found, to adapt the oracles of God to their baseless fictions. (*Against Heresies*, Book 1, Chapter 8, paragraph 1)

By contrast, contemplation of the true shape of Christian belief – which can never be traced apart from constant reference to the person of Jesus Christ – can be a training in knowing what 'fits' and what seems somehow inapposite when proposed as a claim to Christian truth. Those undertaking this training must always remind themselves to look large as well as to peer close – to develop a sensitivity to the integrity of the whole and not just of individual pieces of the picture. And of course, the training never ends, and no individual has unerring judgement about it. It needs a community of people who pray, serve and study together: who are disciples of Christ, in the power of the Holy Spirit.

The breadth of this discerning community is witnessed to nicely in the range of ecclesial traditions represented by the authors of this volume, encompassing Anglicanism, Roman Catholicism, Orthodoxy, and Quakerism. The persuasive power of historic orthodoxy is acknowledged in all these traditions, and others too, and the variety of the authors' backgrounds is evidence that the conciliar statements which have united the Church historically can and do unite it still – even across very significant denominational boundaries. That said, all the authors would I think recognize that the discerning of heresies and the construction of conciliar statements is not in itself a safeguard of unity, but a way to deepen a unity which is ultimately God's gift alone. The activity of distinguishing heresy from orthodoxy is not adequately understood if understood only as a tool for ecclesial social integration; the purpose of the activity is to help believers to love God better, and to be better Christians in the world. It is for this reason that Chapter 12 gives a more positive celebration of what orthodoxy is for: our transfiguring illumination as creatures in relationship with God the Holy and Triune One; our advance from glory to glory.

Before concluding these introductory words, it is important to admit that, notwithstanding the ire they elicit from Irenaeus and others down the ages, heresies (and heretics) aren't *all* bad. Even if we grant that too often heretics allowed a good point they wanted to make to get out of proportion, and to have a deforming effect on the larger picture painted by Christian teaching as a whole, nevertheless it may already have begun to become clear that many heresies were sincerely proffered as attempts to clarify the belief of the Church and inform the lives of believers. Many of those who proffered them regarded themselves as orthodox and catholic believers. We can afford to listen to them generously in many cases. They are the losers in the history of Christian doctrine, and the victors, as Marcus Plested will remind us in his chapter, usually write the history books in a way that is unfavourable to those they have beaten. So heresies often haven't been given an entirely fair press. And just as what we call dirt is often something capable of being useful except for the unfortunate fact that it has turned up in the wrong place – and just as what a mother calls mud on her child's sports kit while reaching for the washing powder is something a gardener would call soil and grow things in – so heresies often had some good points to make. The problem is they didn't always do so in the right way or in an appropriate context. Or in a good number of fascinating cases – high-lighted in the chapters that follow – they just *didn't go far enough*. Heretics have often been shy of the full radicalness of orthodox Christianity, such that their alternatives have been almost rather common-sensical by comparison. All of the first three authors in the book use words like 'radical', 'amazing' and 'shocking' – and use them of *orthodoxy* not of *heresy*. This puts paid to any idea that orthodox belief is some sort of easy way out of intellectual hard work; heresy is more often the easier option.

The generous contention of most authors in this book is that the Church, and orthodox believers, have reason to be grateful to heresies because they have forced us to think our belief out more deeply and thoroughly – whether by their misguided attempts to clarify it, or by challenging it. They have been provocative stimuli, catalysts for energetic thought. Indeed, it was in this generous spirit that the following book had its first origins. Appreciative inquisitiveness was the premise for devoting a term-full of sermons in Peterhouse Chapel, Cambridge (where the editors of this volume serve as Anglican priests) to great heresies, and the majority of essays in this volume were first delivered as sermons in that series – intended not to be excessively encumbered with scholarly apparatus, but to be informed and accessible accounts of how these ancient debates still have much to say to Christians today as they try to make sense of their faith in thought, word and deed. The huge interest in the sermons took us by surprise, and the idea was hatched of making them available to a wider audience by publishing them in a book.

The positively instructive aspect of heresies can perhaps best be compared to the value of parodies in literature or art. This is to offer a counterbalance to Irenaeus's image of the mosaicized fox and king, whereby the rearrangement of pieces to form the fox makes it simply impossible to see that there was ever a king there beforehand. By contrast, we can learn a lot from parodies about the original being parodied, and come to appreciate it in new ways. Heresies are a bit like this: closely imitative of the real thing, forcing us to ask what makes the real thing real and the parody a parody. They are examples of what Rowan Williams in his essay 'Making it Strange' has called 'near-misses' of religious utterance (in Jeremy Begbie's *Sounding the Depths: Theology Through the Arts*, 2002), and such near-misses can be valuable. To see something translated into a different framework and then to ask what has significantly changed for better or for worse is a way of heightening one's pitch of attention to what is under one's nose and assumed to be normative for most of the time. And our appreciation of some things can best be enhanced through contrasts (think of Paul's famous passage on love in 1 Corinthians 13, which is a tour de force of statements of what love is *not* before it declares what love positively *is*).

The language of orthodoxy, as of piety, can be used thoughtlessly when faced with difficult questions, as a stock way to answer, neutralize or suppress them. Perhaps this is evidence of a sort of laziness. Or perhaps the instinct at work is to offset a perceived danger (the danger of being unsettled in one's faith, or lured from the right path). But the killing of lively thought is a much greater danger. In the end a thoughtless recycling of 'what the Church says' will make the narratives and doctrines of orthodoxy stale. As Rowan Williams suggests, 'perhaps theology . . . needs excursions into the mirror-world of what it is *not* saying in order to find out what it *is* about'. Things that are vaguely taken for granted need to be made strange – to be made 'something of a question' – in order that full-blooded orthodoxy may retrieve itself again. 'Mere incorporation in the orthodox Christian fold' will not neutralize all the dangers, or make the questions go away.

This book aims to contribute to such liveliness of thought, to assist the 'avoidance' of heresy not just through strategies of denial and censure, but through adventurous detours through the 'what-ifs?' proposed by orthodoxy's ancient debating partners, so that the pitfalls and limitations of heresies can be better appreciated, and orthodoxy more wholeheartedly celebrated. Such adventures open up the breathtaking hinterland of the dry-seeming formulations of orthodoxy; they reawaken us to the fact that the Creeds (the Church's official statements of belief) that we recite, and the definitions that have been handed down to us from the early Church Councils – some of the most important of which are laid out in the next few pages – are the product of an intense drama. Such adventures in the hinterland reveal the hidden voices in the history of Christian doctrine, and, it is hoped, display what John Sweet in his chapter calls 'the fascination and excitement of the full story'.

The Apostles' Creed, the Nicene Creed, and the Chalcedonian Definition

The Apostles' Creed

The so-called 'Apostles' Creed' is an elaborated version of the 'Old Roman Creed' which is known to have been in use at the end of the second century as a formula of belief recited by those receiving baptism. The earliest surviving Latin text is found in the writings of Priminius, the first abbot of Reichenau, dating from between 710 and 724. The version that follows comes from the English Book of Common Prayer (1662):

> I believe in God the Father Almighty,
> Maker of heaven and earth:
>
> And in Jesus Christ,
> his only Son, our Lord,
> Who was conceived by the Holy Ghost,
> Born of the Virgin Mary,
> Suffered under Pontius Pilate,
> Was crucified, dead, and buried:
> He descended into hell;
> The third day he rose again from the dead;
> He ascended into heaven,
> And sitteth on the right hand of God the Father Almighty;
> From thence he shall come to judge the quick and the dead.
>
> I believe in the Holy Ghost;
> The holy Catholick Church;
> The Communion of Saints;
> The Forgiveness of sins:
> The Resurrection of the body,
> And the life everlasting.
> Amen.

The Nicene Creed

The Niceno-Constantinopolitan Creed (more commonly called the Nicene Creed) dates from the Second Ecumenical Council of Constantinople, held in 381. It builds on an earlier Creed formulated by the First Ecumenical Council, held at Nicea in 325. The version given here is again from the English Book of Common Prayer (1662).

I believe in one God the Father Almighty, Maker of heaven and earth, And of all things visible and invisible:

And in one Lord Jesus Christ, the only-begotten Son of God, Begotten of his Father before all worlds, God of God, Light of Light, Very God of very God, Begotten, not made, Being of one substance [*homoousios*] with the Father, By whom all things were made: Who for us men and for our salvation came down from heaven, And was incarnate by the Holy Ghost of the Virgin Mary, And was made man, And was crucified also for us under Pontius Pilate. He suffered and was buried, And the third day he rose again according to the Scriptures, And ascended into heaven, And sitteth on the right hand of the Father. And he shall come again with glory to judge both the quick and the dead: Whose kingdom shall have no end.

And I believe in the Holy Ghost, The Lord and giver of life, Who proceedeth from the Father and the Son, Who with the Father and the Son together is worshipped and glorified, Who spake by the Prophets. And I believe one Catholick and Apostolick Church. I acknowledge one Baptism for the remission of sins. And I look for the Resurrection of the dead, And the life of the world to come. Amen.

The Chalcedonian Definition

The Fourth Ecumenical Council, held at Chalcedon in 451, declared the following to be consistent with orthodox Christian belief; it has become known as the 'Chalcedonian Definition':

> Following the holy fathers, we all with one accord teach men to acknowledge one and the same Son, our Lord Jesus Christ, at once complete in Godhead and complete in manhood, truly God and truly man, consisting also of a reasonable soul and body; of one substance [*homoousios*] with the Father as regards his Godhead, and at the same time of one substance with us as regards his manhood; like us in all respects, apart from sin; as regards his Godhead, begotten of the Father before the ages, but yet as regards his manhood begotten, for us men and for our salvation, of Mary the Virgin, the God-bearer [*theotokos*]; one and the same Christ, Son, Lord, Only-begotten, recognized in two natures, without confusion, without change, without division, without separation; the distinction of natures being in no way annulled by the union, but rather the characteristics of each nature being preserved and coming together to form one person and subsistence [*hypostasis*], not as parted or separated into two persons, but one and the same Son and Only-begotten God the Word, Lord Jesus Christ; even as the prophets from earliest times spoke of him, and our Lord Jesus Christ himself taught us, and the creed of the fathers has handed down to us.

Part 1

HERESIES OF THE PERSON OF CHRIST
AND HOW TO AVOID THEM

1

Arianism:
Is Jesus Christ divine and
eternal or was he created?

MICHAEL B. THOMPSON

———•◆•———

What is Arianism?

Arianism is the heresy which denies the full divinity of Jesus
Christ. It is named after Arius, who was born about 270 and
died in 336. He was a priest in charge of one of the principal
churches at Alexandria and he appears to have believed that the
Son of God was not eternal but was created before the ages
by the Father as an instrument for the making of the world.
Arius's teaching was opposed chiefly by Athanasius, a deacon
at Alexandria, and was eventually condemned by the First
Ecumenical Council, held at Nicea in 325. It became an article
of 'Nicene' orthodoxy that the Father and the Son were
equally eternal, and the famous term *homoousios* ('of the same
substance') was used to express this belief.

*   *   *

Key Scriptures

Have this mind among yourselves, which was in Christ Jesus, who,
though he was in the form of God, did not count equality with
God a thing to be grasped, but emptied himself, taking the form
of a servant, being born in the likeness of men. And being found
in human form he humbled himself and became obedient unto death,

even death on a cross. Therefore God has highly exalted him and bestowed on him the name which is above every name, that at the name of Jesus every knee should bow, in heaven and earth and under the earth, and every tongue confess that Jesus Christ is Lord, to the glory of God the Father. (Philippians 2.5–11)

Jesus came and stood among them and said to them, 'Peace be with you.' When he had said this, he showed them his hands and his side. Then the disciples were glad when they saw the Lord. Jesus said to them again, 'Peace be with you. As the Father has sent me, even so I send you.' And when he had said this, he breathed on them, and said to them, 'Receive the Holy Spirit. If you forgive the sins of any, they are forgiven; if you retain the sins of any, they are retained.'

Now Thomas, one of the twelve, called the Twin, was not with them when Jesus came. So the other disciples told him, 'We have seen the Lord.' But he said to them, 'Unless I see in his hands the print of the nails, and place my finger in the mark of the nails, and place my hand in his side, I will not believe.'

Eight days later, his disciples were again in the house, and Thomas was with them. The doors were shut, but Jesus came and stood among them, and said, 'Peace be with you.' Then he said to Thomas, 'Put your finger here, and see my hands; and put out your hand, and place it in my side; do not be faithless, but believing.' Thomas answered him, 'My Lord and my God!' Jesus said to him, 'Have you believed because you have seen me? Blessed are those who have not seen and yet believe.' (John 20.19b–29)

*   *   *

In my first term at university 35 years ago, I was invited to a Bible study. I'd never been to one before; I hadn't been to church for ages, and I didn't know what to expect. At one point in the meeting, I came face to face with the Christian claim that Jesus was fully human and fully divine. And for the first time in my life, I stopped to think about it. I decided I couldn't believe that, so I walked out of the group in the middle of their study.

My problem was with the notion that a man could be God. Arius's problem was more the other way around – how could God in all his fullness become a man?

Unlike me, Arius started from a position of strong faith and orthodoxy; he was a well-educated presbyter in one of the leading churches in Alexandria at the beginning of the fourth century. He reacted against what he perceived to be the heretical teaching that left no room for distinguishing the divinity of God the Father from that of God the Son, for if there was no such distinction wouldn't the limitations of the incarnate Son (God the Son made human in the person of Jesus Christ) have to be ascribed to the Father as well? Arius also wanted to preserve the sharp distinction between creator and creation. Above all, like later Muslims and Unitarians he sought to protect monotheism and the unity of God.

The issue for Arius was, simply, this: how could God, the unknowable, immutable, transcendent one, become fully human without being changed in the process? Driving the question for him was a strong Neoplatonic cosmology that sharply distinguished between an unchanging, heavenly sphere of existence and the changeable created order. This dualistic philosophical starting point, together with an assumption that monotheism could allow no distinction between a Father and Son within God, ultimately led him to press certain biblical passages over against others. Arius minimized the teachings of some scriptural texts in order to produce a version of Christianity more consistent with his presuppositions. In the process, orthodoxy was sacrificed on the altar of philosophy.

Even though he gets a lot of bad press, Arius was, as far as we can tell, scrupulous and careful in his study of the Bible. Like many others before and after him, he was struck by passages which could imply that in one way or another the Son of God was limited or was subordinate to the Father. After all, didn't Jesus say, 'Why do you ask me about what is good? One there

17

is who is good' (Matthew 19.17)? And in John's Gospel didn't he say, 'the Father is greater than I' (John 14.28)? The fact that Jesus prayed to God seemed to imply inferiority: how could one who was co-equal with the Father pray, 'not my will but thine be done' (Luke 22.42)? Surely the man who hungered, thirsted, slept and wept, suffered and died could not have shared directly in the very essence of God. It's not what we'd expect, much less fully comprehend.

Arius didn't deny the Fourth Gospel's teaching that 'in the beginning was the Word' and 'the Word was God' (John 1.1). He could still say that the Son was both human and even, in a sense, 'divine', but he qualified that assertion in a crucial way: the divine Word that existed before all creation was himself also created. According to Socrates (*c.* 380–*c.* 439), an early Church historian, Arius put it in the following nutshell: 'There was when he was not.'

Instead of pre-existing for all eternity with the Father, the Word had a beginning before himself going on to create the world and become a man. He was therefore a lesser, inferior deity, a 'demiurge', close in some ways but exterior to God himself. The *Logos* (the Greek word that John uses in his Gospel and that is translated into English as 'Word') was a creature who, precisely because he was created and begotten, could not fully know or comprehend the mind of God. In other words, Jesus was fully human, but not fully God.

Arius combined this basic distinction with something no orthodox Christian would dispute – a great ethical emphasis on moral advancement through obedience, after the example of Jesus. But the logic of Arian teaching meant that Jesus, the perfect creature, only *models* for us the way to salvation. We follow his example in order to learn how to win grace and to achieve for ourselves deliverance from our predicament. Arius appealed to the people of his day because he was a stubborn man of principle with strong ascetic discipline, impressive in appearance, confident and persuasive in his speech. There was something very attractive about such a noble religion which protected God's unity and transcendence and which upheld human effort and perseverance in the manner of the Stoics (those Greek philosophers who taught self-control and detachment). Knowing that what people sing influences what they believe, Arius set his ideas to verse in a composition called the *Thalia* so that his followers could more easily remember his teachings. This sensible blend of philosophy, theology and exegesis almost won the day.

But Alexander, Arius's bishop, disagreed, and so did Athanasius, a local deacon, who distinguished between 'generation' and 'creation'. The Son, Athanasius said, was *generated*, begotten by God from eternity, but he had no beginning. This generation was eternal and internal to God, whereas creation was in time and external to God. The Son was therefore *homoousios* (being of the same substance) and co-eternal with the Father, not simply *homoiousios* (being of similar substance to God) as some of the Arians claimed. The only difference between those two Greek words is the letter 'iota'. But it is the difference between Christ being God and Christ being like God.

In the year 325 the Council of Nicea rejected Arianism and put the words into the creed we say today: 'very God of very God, begotten, not made, being of one substance with the Father' (see p. 11). That did not settle the issue. The Arian controversy continued until the language of the Nicene creed became widely established in 381 by the time of the Council of Constantinople.

So what? What's really at stake? Isn't this splitting hairs over a dogma, a fine point for theologians to debate in seminars? Well, folk on the street don't decide their Christology with an iota any more (if they have a Christology), and belief in a demiurge doesn't preoccupy the average grocery-shopper. But most people outside the Church, and quite a few within, don't believe that Jesus Christ was and is the one and only God before whom one day every knee will bow, to the glory of the

Father. For many he remains simply a great moral teacher and example.

If Arianism is right it makes a difference in many ways; I'll mention briefly three. First, God did not send a creature in order to show us how we could bridge the gap between heaven and earth by learning how to follow a wonderful example. Both the human predicament and the divine solution are far more profound than that. It's the difference between a religion that simply says to us 'try harder', and the belief that God is the one who has done what it takes to deliver us, through the incarnation and the cross. As one of my students put it, the Son cannot be a bridge between God and humanity if the bridge doesn't fully reach to both ends. The nature of Christ directly affects how we can be restored and put right with God.

Second, revelation is also at stake. Arianism denied that God the unknowable can be known; even the Logos didn't have perfect knowledge of God because, as a mere creature, he was separate from the divine being. In orthodox Christianity, however, Christ offers us not secondhand, indirect knowledge, but the direct experience of relationship with the eternal God who calls us to know him. If Arius was right, the love we find in Christ (and by analogy, what we experience in the Spirit) is really external to that God. If Christ does not fully know God, can we fully trust him to deliver us?

Third, why should we want to emulate, much less to praise, the God of Arius? This God does not give of himself, but sends a lesser, created being to show kindness. God remains an isolated, insulated ruler who cannot involve himself intimately with his creation. Orthodoxy is far more radical (and personal) than that!

The texts cited by the Arians certainly remind us that, in so far as the Son was fully human, he did experience all of the weakness and limitations we know, yet without sin. None of these texts however addresses or denies the divine essence of the Son. For each of them there are other passages that reflect belief in the full deity of Christ (such as John 1.1, 18; 1 Corinthians 8.6; Colossians 1.15–20; 2.9; Titus 2.13; Romans 9.5) – texts by Jewish Christians who did not compromise their monotheistic faith. The biblical writers were apparently not that interested in speculations about the metaphysics of ontology (the science of being); they focused on the concrete reality that they experienced in the person of Jesus.

In the passage from Philippians 2 at the head of this chapter we catch a glimpse of the early belief in the pre-existence of the Son as deity when Paul says, 'who, though he was in the form of God, did not count equality with God a thing to be grasped' (Philippians 2.6). That belief is consistent with what we find in other New Testament texts, for example, John 1.1f., 14; 2 Corinthians 8.9; Galatians 4.4. But the main point in Philippians is precisely the wonder that Christ emptied himself in humiliation, even to the shame of death on a cross. The eternal Son did not take advantage of his status, but poured himself out in obedience for our sake. The magnitude of such a sacrifice may be something we cannot fathom, but it fully coheres with the very nature of our self-giving God.

Paul goes on to say that this man, whose obedience won our life, has been given the name which is above every name (Philippians 2.9–11). That name is not Jesus, as some popular choruses assume. 'Jesus' or 'Yeshua' was simply a form of 'Joshua', a very common name in his day. The given name that Paul refers to is the tetragrammaton (YHWH) revealed in the Old Testament, the sacred name of God, the four consonants which orthodox Jews do not dare to speak for its holiness and which most Bibles print as 'Lord'.

What is particularly striking here in Philippians 2.9–11 is the way that Paul combines two Old Testament passages, both of them from Isaiah. Isaiah 45.22–23 reads: 'Turn to me and be saved, all the ends of the earth! For I am God, and there is no other. By myself I have sworn, from my mouth has gone forth in righteousness a word that shall not return: "To me every knee shall bow, every tongue shall swear."' Six times in that same chapter of Isaiah comes the refrain about God, 'There is no other' (verses 5, 6, 14, 18, 21, 22), emphasizing his uniqueness.

The second passage comes from Isaiah 42.8: 'I am the LORD, that is my name. My glory I give to no other.' Paul in his letter to the Philippians is applying some of the strongest affirmations about the unique sovereignty and identity of God in the Old Testament to the person of Jesus Christ, before whom every knee will bow in worship. This sort of adoration and authority belongs to no mere creature, not even an angel.

That brings us to John 20.19b–29 (also quoted at the head of this chapter), the resurrection appearance in the upper room. I like Thomas, the questioning, doubting disciple. In John's Gospel he's apparently an intelligent, thoughtful man, not wishy-washy but loyal to what he knows to be true. Like a good scholar, he doesn't want his information secondhand, but insists on getting the facts from the primary source. He has the stubbornness of Arius, but he lacks the arrogance.

When Christ appears to Thomas in the climactic scene of the Gospel, this doubter makes the simplest and most direct affirmation of the deity of Christ one could ask for: 'My Lord and my God!' (John 20.28). It doesn't get much clearer than that, especially when we recognize that this passage is one half of an *inclusio* (or bracketing), the other half being the Johannine prologue. Together, like bookends, these verses emphasize the identity of Christ (1.1; 20.28). Who Jesus is makes all the difference in the world.

So what's the best way to avoid Arianism? How do we maintain faith in the full deity of Jesus? Is it Bible study? That helps as we discover how strong a scriptural case there is for orthodoxy, but it's not the ultimate answer: Arius was a well-trained exegete with a keen eye for detail. In fact, he led two weekly Bible studies, on Wednesdays and Fridays.

Is the best preventative a 'consistent' theology? A consistently high view of God's sovereignty is part of what led to Arius's conclusions in the first place. Our presuppositions, the ideas we bring to a discussion of what God is like, can keep us from discovering the fullness of his self-revelation in the person of Christ. Upholding both the full humanity and deity of Jesus is no less important than maintaining the trinity and unity of God, divine sovereignty and human responsibility, justification by grace and judgement according to works, and a host of other apparent paradoxes that we may be tempted to resolve by emphasizing one side of the truth over another. To demand philosophical 'consistency' is to carve the reality of God down to fit within our small world of thought, rather than to allow his revelation to stand and reform our own thinking.

I think the best defence against Arianism is precisely what hastened the development of a high Christology in the earliest Church – real, personal encounter with the risen Christ, and attentive participation in a worshipping community. Meeting Jesus and reflecting together with others on what he has accomplished for us makes us want to worship him. It's hard to worship a mere man, or even a demiurge.

As I was leaving that Bible study so long ago, a girl in the group said to me, 'The next time we meet, you'll believe.' She was right. A few weeks later, I came to faith. Not because I had sorted out some syllogisms or developed a watertight philosophical system or exegeted my way into orthodoxy. No, someone had simply shared the gospel with me, helping me to see that, in Christ, God had come to do for me what I could never do for myself. He fully bridged the chasm that separated us, died to deal with my sins, and brought me back to himself. My natural instinct was to thank him, to praise him, and to worship him in the company of other Christians from whom I could learn more of my new faith. And I found that as a result I had no problem with the deity of Christ. I can't pretend that I can get my mind fully around that doctrine. If I did, I guess I'd be God. But I believe it.

2

Docetism:
Is Jesus Christ really human or
did he just appear to be so?

JOHN SWEET

What is Docetism?

Docetism is the heresy which denies the full humanity of Jesus
Christ. The name comes from the Greek verb *dokein*, which
means 'to seem': Docetists hold that Jesus only seemed to be
human. This belief became particularly prominent in the second
century, especially among the Gnostics (for more on whom see
Chapter 10), but was a tendency in theological thought rather
than a fully formulated doctrine, which helps explain why it is
not named after an individual. However, by the fourth century
this tendency led one Apollinarius of Laodicea (*c.* 310–*c.* 390)
explicitly to deny that Jesus possessed a human mind or
soul, and this particular kind of Docetism became known as
Apollinarianism. It was ruled to be heretical by the Second
Ecumenical Council, held at Constantinople in 381.

*   *   *

Key Scriptures

Then God said, 'Let us make man in our image, after our likeness; and let them have dominion over the fish of the sea, and
over the birds of the air, and over the cattle, and over all the earth,
and over every creeping thing that creeps upon the earth.' So God

created man in his own image, in the image of God he created him; male and female he created them. (Genesis 1.26–27)

In the days of his flesh, Jesus offered up prayers and supplications, with loud cries and tears, to him who was able to save him from death, and he was heard for his godly fear. Although he was a Son, he learned obedience through what he suffered; and being made perfect, he became the source of eternal salvation to all who obey him. (Hebrews 5.7–9)

* * *

Most heresies look all right and have a degree of truth in them, or else they would not catch on. But as we all know, appearances can be deceptive. Docetism has much to do with appearances: the word comes from the Greek verb meaning 'to seem' or 'to appear'. If many Jews (like all Arians) found it hard to believe that the man Jesus was really God, for many Greeks it was even harder to believe that the Christ they worshipped as God could have been really human. Might he have just *appeared* to be human?

The Greek philosophy current in the early centuries of the Christian Church, a philosophy stemming from Plato, distinguished radically between appearance and reality, flesh and spirit. Matter, for them, was transitory, unreal, even evil; the body was a tomb, and the spirit escaped it at death. Through philosophy or knowledge (*gnosis*), you might be set free even before death. Gnosticism (see Chapter 10) was often bound up with oriental views of matter: the body as inherently impure, unclean. For God to be human, to be mixed up in matter – that was demeaning, disgusting, unthinkable to the Greek mind; and for God to suffer was a contradiction in terms. There were two stories told to get round these problems.

First, Jesus appeared to be human but was really a phantasm – just as in one story Helen never went to Troy, it was merely a lookalike phantom. But there was not much mileage in that: it was too well known that Jesus was a real man and died a horribly real death under Pontius Pilate.

There was a second, more plausible story that said that Jesus was indeed truly human and that only at his baptism did the divine Christ-Spirit enter into him (this is Adoptionism, see Chapter 5). This divine Spirit enabled his powerful words and deeds, and it left him, returning to the Father, before the man Jesus was crucified.

For people of this outlook it was the words that mattered, not the human mouthpiece. It was the truth that set you free, that opened your eyes to the real world of the spirit. For them salvation was not about healing the whole person, body and spirit, but about escaping from the body; 'resurrection' was a metaphor for this escape through enlightenment. In no sense could the human Jesus be divine, or the Christ-Spirit be human.

There are phrases in the New Testament that a Gnostic could read in this way, like the little hymn – 'Awake, O sleeper, and arise from the dead, and Christ shall give you light' – quoted in Ephesians 5.14. But the New Testament writers were not Gnostics; they believed that Jesus was God with us, Immanuel, bone of our bone, flesh of our flesh. He was born of a woman, and took human flesh to heal and save it. He grew and learned, as we do. The passage from the Letter to the Hebrews quoted at the head of this chapter is evidence of this: 'In the days of his flesh, Jesus offered up prayers and supplications, with loud cries and tears . . . Although he was a Son, he learned obedience through what he suffered; and being made perfect he became the source of eternal salvation to all who obey him' (Hebrews 5.7–9). Christ lifted up our humanity with his. In the words of Irenaeus in the second century, Jesus Christ 'did . . . become what we are, that he might bring us to be even what he is himself' – words which are sometimes paraphrased: 'He became man that we might become God' (see the preface to Book V of *Against Heresies*).

Are people in danger of Docetism today? Not the 'Jesus as a phantasm' kind. Nor the 'Jesus as a temporary vehicle for the divine Christ-Spirit' kind. But there is a third kind, a more subtle and scriptural kind. When you read John's Gospel it's hard not to see Jesus as omniscient, in total control. He knew what was in man and didn't need anyone to tell him; he claimed to have come down from heaven and to be on his way back; he did eye-stretching miracles: changed 150 gallons of water into wine; raised Lazarus four days dead. And he made a series of I am pronouncements – most notably, 'Before Abraham was, I am' (John 8.58) – the divine name revealed to Moses at the burning bush. John, of course, presents Jesus and his story in a strikingly different way and different idiom from Matthew, Mark and Luke: his concern was to affirm that Jesus was not just human but truly God with us. In his Letters, on the other hand, he explicitly guards against those who deny that Jesus has come 'in the flesh' (1 John 4.2; 2 John 7). But to John's readers now, how truly human is the Jesus he presents both in his Gospel and in his Letters? Jesus's flesh may be human, but is his mind?

This question came to a head with the fourth-century theologian Apollinarius of Laodicea. He was a friend of Athanasius, the great defender against Arius of Christ's divinity. Apollinarius thought he was simply restating traditional orthodoxy: he believed, like many before him, that Jesus was truly 'flesh', God incarnate, but with the divine Logos (Word) as his mind. He was quite clear that Jesus did not have a human mind, did not learn and develop morally, could not have been humanly ignorant. He explained away passages like 'about that day, no one knows, neither the angels in heaven, nor the Son, but only the Father' (Mark 13.32).

Apollinarius was genuinely concerned for our salvation: if Jesus was not fully divine, how could he give us the divine life to share? The orthodox were equally concerned: what use to us is Jesus if he was only human from the neck down (so to speak), if he did not assume a human mind? 'What he did not assume he did not heal' was their mantra. When people talk about Docetism today they mean any tendency to underplay the full humanness of Jesus, in favour of his divinity.

Two questions then. How can we avoid Docetism? What does it matter?

In answer to the first question, I would say: draw on the whole Bible, not selected passages, and read it with the same critical attention you'd give to any important text. (To say you mustn't treat the Holy Bible like that, is itself a form of Docetism, as if God's word can only reach us bypassing the human mind.)

If you start not with John, but Mark, the earliest Gospel, you find a palpably human Jesus. He refers to himself as a prophet; he fends off laudatory titles, and calls himself simply 'son of man', man created in God's image, as in Psalm 8. He plays down his healings. In Gethsemane he is genuinely, agonizingly confused: 'Abba, Father . . . remove this cup from me; yet not what I will, but what thou wilt' (Mark 14.36). And on the cross: 'My God, my God, why hast thou forsaken me?' (Mark 15.34).

But all the Gospels, including Mark's, tell the story, so to say, bifocally. Behind Jesus and his contemporaries in Palestine you can see the people of Mark's or Matthew's or Luke's or John's church; and they tell the story so as to hint at what they now know this man Jesus really was, and is. Or in John's case, not just hint but make it quite explicit: I AM. But never for a moment forgetting that Jesus really was human – like the Letter to the Hebrews, which begins by hailing Jesus as the divine wisdom incarnate, but goes on to insist on his learning through suffering.

Second, as a way to avoid downplaying Christ's humanity, honour Jesus's parents, not just Mary – divine conception for some may seem to compromise his full humanity – but Joseph too. In becoming fully human aren't parents, as role models, and the society we grow up in, more important than genetics?

So pay attention too to the Old Testament: it was the Scriptures, the story of Israel, the story he learnt from parents and synagogue that shaped all he did. Otherwise it's easy to think like Marcion (see Chapter 7) that Jesus owed nothing to his surroundings, being programmed directly by the Heavenly Father.

But how could he be really man and really God? My third suggestion for avoiding Docetism is: have a higher view of humanity and the body so that it's not demeaning to God who, as Genesis 1.26–27 reminds us, made humankind in his own image and likeness. Or rather think more highly not of what we are now, which has sadly become so unlike the image of our maker, but of what God has made us to be in the future: 'Beloved, we are God's children now; it does not yet appear what we shall be, but we know that when he appears we shall be like him, for we shall see him as he is' (1 John 3.2). William Blake puts it provocatively in his poem 'The Everlasting Gospel', when he has God say: 'Thou art a man: God is no more: / Thy own humanity learn to adore, / For that is My spirit of life.' 'God is no more' means the false god, what Paul calls 'the god of this age'; Blake calls him '*Nobodaddy*'.

If this is too much for you, my fourth suggestion is: try thinking in verbs, rather than nouns. The Hebrews thought primarily in terms of activity, of doing; Greeks in terms of being ('ontology'). 'God' and 'man' as nouns are like East and West, never the twain shall meet. God's being is utterly beyond ours. But God is a doer, a maker, a lover, and we can be his learners, his apprentices, as Jesus described himself. In John 5 the Jews attack Jesus because he 'called God his Father, making himself equal with God' (v. 18). Jesus replies, 'The Son can do nothing of his own accord, but only what he sees the Father doing . . . The Father loves the Son, and shows him all that he himself is doing' (vv. 19–20) – the craftsman-father shows his apprentice-son all the art and mystery of his craft; the son watches and listens; he learns obedience through what he suffers (Hebrews 5.8); and will be given even greater things to do. In the upper room Jesus tells *his* apprentices that they in turn will do greater works, because he goes to the Father (John 14.12) – and his spirit will be with them and in them. As Irenaeus said: 'He became man that we might become God.' In terms of 'doing' and 'loving', Irenaeus's words become a bit more thinkable. It's still a vital part of Eastern Orthodoxy. We in the West need to recover it.

Another suggestion which follows is 'think relationally', in terms of relationships: God with us. We are members one of another 'in Adam'; in Christ, the second Adam, we are united with his Father; and the Holy Spirit is the active, loving power that binds us together.

A final suggestion is to adopt what John Keats calls 'negative capability'. Too strenuously avoiding one heresy may land you, like Apollinarius, in another. No formula can explain entirely satisfactorily how Jesus can be both human and divine. It's mystery. So accept it with Keatsian 'negative capability', the capacity for 'being in uncertainties, mysteries, doubts, without any irritable reaching after fact and reason' (letter to George and Thomas Keats, dated Sunday 21 December 1817).

And now to the second of our two questions: does it matter, Jesus being really, fully human? What practical difference does it make?

It makes a difference to how you see and treat others, especially those who are distasteful, or hostile, or even evil. Aren't we all, like heresies, a mixture of good and bad? Remember Matthew 25 and Jesus's words at the Judgement to the sheep and goats: 'In as much as you have cared – or failed to care – for one of the least of my brethren, you have done it, or failed to do it, to me' (a paraphrase of Matthew 25.40 and 45 conflated). What weight have those words if he is not truly one of us, bone of our bone, flesh of our flesh, so that good and bad people alike are his siblings, and ours?

It makes a difference, too, to how you look at yourself, body as well as mind. Sometimes it's harder to love ourselves than to love others: we can feel ashamed of ourselves, fed up with ourselves. But Jesus is more than an example, more than a sin-bearer: he's a brother. Paul describes Jesus as the eldest among a large family of brothers (see Romans 8.29). We share his relationship with God as beloved children, fellow apprentices learning the Father's mystery, learning to be divine. He became man that we might become God, united with God in love, as he is.

Of course ontologically that won't do. 'Man' is not 'God' – it's arrogance to claim it. Jesus is more than human; we are less than divine. But relationally, thinking in relationship terms, aren't we to him as siblings are to their elder brothers, or as children are to their parents? This is the relationship that we, with Jesus, already enjoy. Taught by him we are bold to say, 'Abba, Father'. This relationship we will finally – at the end of a very long learning curve – enjoy to the full.

'He became man that we might become God.' Was Irenaeus right? How dare we, ugly ducklings, dust and ashes, think such thoughts? Christian doctrine has its list of heresies, danger areas to be marked off, but the aim is to leave clear the fascination and excitement of the full story. Irenaeus may seem impossibly presumptuous, and we may feel more comfortable with a humbler, more 'realistic' view of ourselves, but isn't this thrilling, mind-blowing, something to shout about? I have to pinch myself to remember just how amazing the Christian faith is. And when I do, the words of the hymn 'Jerusalem the golden' come to mind:

> Exult, O dust and ashes!
> > The Lord shall be thy part.
> His only, his for ever,
> > Thou shalt be, and thou art!

3

Nestorianism:
Is Jesus Christ one person or does he have a split identity, with his divine nature separate and divided from his human nature?

A. N. WILLIAMS

What is Nestorianism?

Nestorianism is the heresy which denies that Christ was a single person, at once God and man. It is named after Nestorius, patriarch of Constantinople, who was born some time after 351 and died some time after 451. He objected to the use of the term *theotokos* (God-bearer) as a title for the Virgin Mary because he thought it suggested an Apollinarian denial of Jesus's full humanity (see Chapter 2). Nestorius was opposed chiefly by Cyril, patriarch of Alexandria, and his teaching was condemned by the Third Ecumenical Council, held at Ephesus in the year 431.

* * *

Key Scriptures

In the beginning was the Word, and the Word was with God, and the Word was God. He was in the beginning with God; all things were made through him, and without him was not anything made that was made. In him was life, and the life was the light of men. The light shines in the darkness, and the darkness has not overcome it.

There was a man sent from God, whose name was John. He came for testimony, to bear witness to the light, that all might believe through him. He was not the light, but came to bear witness to the light.

The true light that enlightens every man was coming into the world. He was in the world, and the world was made through him, yet the world knew him not. He came to his own home, and his own people received him not. But to all who received him, who believed in his name, he gave power to become children of God; who were born, not of blood nor of the will of the flesh nor of the will of man, but of God.

And the Word became flesh and dwelt among us, full of grace and truth; we have beheld his glory, glory as of the only Son from the Father. (John 1.1–14)

I mean that the heir, as long as he is a child, is no better than a slave, though he is the owner of all the estate; but he is under guardians and trustees until the date set by the father. So with us; when we were children, we were slaves to the elemental spirits of the universe. But when the time had fully come, God sent forth his Son, born of woman, born under the law, to redeem those who were under the law, so that we might receive adoption as sons. And because you are sons, God has sent the Spirit of his Son into our hearts, crying, 'Abba! Father!' So through God you are no longer a slave but a son, and if a son then an heir. (Galatians 4.1–7)

Do not invite death by the error of your life, nor bring on destruction by the works of your hands; because God did not make death, and he does not delight in the death of the living. For he created all things that they might exist, and the generative forces of the world are wholesome, and there is no destructive poison in them; and the dominion of Hades is not on earth. For righteousness is immortal. (Wisdom 1.12–15)

*   *   *

There is an order to heresies, as there is an order to orthodoxy. There is also, in an odd way, a positive side to heresies if we allow our knowledge of them to steer us, not just away from error, but into the arms of the one who is the way, the truth and the life, our Lord and Saviour, Jesus Christ. The Church's quest for knowledge of this Lord led it to debate, in fairly rapid succession, four possible portraits of Christ, rejecting each in turn. Each rejected option blacked out an area, and these negative pieces in turn fit together in a kind of puzzle, leaving a space in which the Church drew many faces of Christ down through the centuries, each different, yet each hewing to the broad outline of the community's agreed belief.

The first two heresies concerning this Christ which were condemned by the early Church were Arianism and Apollinarianism (a kind of Docetism), which have been discussed in Chapters 1 and 2 respectively. Together, these condemnations established as the positive content of Christian belief the notion that Jesus Christ had two natures, one fully divine and one fully human. The next two heresies to be condemned departed from this assumption that there are two natures in Christ, and each of these heresies represented an answer to the question of how the two natures are related: Nestorianism and Eutychianism (tackled in Chapter 4) could not have arisen without the earlier condemnations of Arianism and Apollinarianism establishing that there *are* two natures in Christ. The logical ordering of these four heresies concerning Christ's person reflects the process of the Christian community's meditation on the Bible, its slowly being drawn by the Spirit into a greater knowledge of the truth of the Logos, the one through whom creation was ordered and who is logic and reason beyond all we could ever grasp.

The deeper truth about Christ that the condemnations of Nestorianism and Eutychianism established as the positive content of Christian belief was that the divine and human natures in Christ are neither mixed together as Eutychian theology would have it, producing a hybrid which is something else altogether (as green, a mixture of yellow and blue, is nevertheless itself neither yellow nor blue), nor are the two natures divided from one another, each remote from and unaffected by their union. 'Nestorianism' designates this divided view: the notion that Christ has two natures, but that we should think of them as quite separate from one another.

Like most heresies, Nestorianism is grounded in some justifiable worries about the problems in the alternative views. Like most heresies, it is grounded in good theological intentions and genuine piety, for heresies tend precisely not to be mischievous; if anything, they tried to represent views that are too conservative, too wary of believing that what the Father, the Son and the Spirit have done and are still doing with this world surpasses all our wildest imaginings.

The goodness of what the divine persons are about means that, in the first instance, they are to be honoured, not through avoidance of error, but through praise of their holiness. It might be best, therefore, not to think in terms of how to avoid Nestorianism, but rather, how to worship rightly – a theme which will be taken up further in Chapter 12 and in the Epilogue. Trying to avoid heresy may be like setting out down the street with the intention of not stepping on any cracks in the pavement: it will not necessarily keep you from stepping on cracks and, in the meantime, you will have been looking down at concrete when you could have been looking up and around at all the beautiful things that Providence has sent you on this day. That is what it means to say that all the Christological heresies establish a positive content to belief: they are better understood as helping us to know and speak the truth than as warning us away from the mortal perils of saying something wrong. So if the Church's condemnation of Nestorianism tells us we should not speak of Christ's natures as though they were divided from one another, how then should we think and speak? Or to put it another way, what is the positive content of being orthodox in a specifically non-Nestorian way?

We may be helped along the way to right glorification of God if we understand why exactly Nestorius got into trouble. He did not set out to be novel or original, far from it: he saw himself as preserving the integrity of the Christian faith, and he was responding to what he saw as dangerous talk that was being bandied about in his place and time – and it really was dangerous talk. Christian orthodoxy is always dangerous, the immensity of its declarations and implications asking us radically to revise the way we think about the world and act in it as the consequence of our belief. The danger Nestorius saw was that in his time piety had led some to speak of the Blessed Virgin Mary as *theotokos*, which means in Greek 'God-bearer'. There was no doubt that Mary bore someone; the Gospel narratives tell us she was the mother of Jesus of Nazareth and no one was contesting that identity. However, Nestorius thought that to say she was the mother of God was to make a disastrous, if almost imperceptible, leap of logic. On the orthodox account (and Nestorius was trying to safeguard what he saw as orthodoxy), only one of the natures in Christ was human. It follows that only one nature was capable of being born. In Nestorius's view, Mary could be called the mother of Jesus, mother to the human nature in Christ, but she could not be called God's mother. Divine nature, by definition, cannot have a mother. Being eternal, it does not begin to be and it is in the nature of being born that one minute you are not here and the next minute out you pop and you exist as an independent person. According to Nestorius, therefore, you could call Mary the mother of Jesus, but not the mother of God.

Nestorius was patriarch of Constantinople, and that made him pastorally responsible for a great many Christian souls. To allow people to go on thinking in misleading ways about divine nature, to take the uncreated God for something which, like created things, has a beginning, is just about the worst theological mistake you can make. It does not just violate the teaching established by church councils; it violates the second commandment, which prohibits idolatry, that is, mistaking created things for the divine persons. Nestorius was not objecting to the title *theotokos* because it got something wrong about Mary, nor was he objecting to the pious practice of giving honour to her. If that were so, Nestorianism would be a Marian heresy and it is not. Nestorianism is a Christological heresy, a bad misunderstanding of who Christ is, for in denying that Mary was the mother of God, Nestorius was effectively saying that although the two natures of Christ belonged to one person, there was a dividing wall between them: Mary is mother of one half, but not of the other.

An initial way of understanding the problem is to think of a human analogy: I get some of my characteristics from my mother and some from my father. Just because I am like my mother in some respects and my father in others, however, I would not say my mother was mother of parts of me and my father was father of other parts. Mothers and fathers are parents to whole persons, in which all sorts of disparate, perhaps contradictory, elements come together, making the distinct unity that is a human person. It makes little sense to identify a parent as the origin of part of a person, and it makes no more sense to call Mary the mother of part of Jesus Christ. If Jesus Christ is both truly a human person and truly God, then Mary is both the mother of Jesus of Nazareth and the mother of God. If the matter ends there, however, we have gone no further than to establish the correct title for Mary and, as noted earlier, the real issue is not honouring Mary but rightly understanding her Son. So what does Mary's title 'Mother of God' tell us about Christ?

At one level, you can handily avoid Nestorianism simply by wandering around muttering to yourself and anyone else who cares to listen, 'The Virgin Mary is the God-bearer', though you would be missing the point. The real point of the

37

condemnation of Nestorianism is not to affirm that slogan, so much as to affirm the full significance of the prologue to the Gospel of John (1.1–14), which is quoted at the head of this chapter: that was what Nestorius missed. John's prologue tells us that the Word was made flesh and dwelt among us, full of grace and truth, a statement of such huge proportions that it used to be the custom to read the entire first chapter of the Gospel of John at the end of every communion service, and when the reader intoned the words 'and the Word became flesh' (v. 14) all the people would kneel, from the sheer wonder of it. These words, along with 'Glory be to the Father and to the Son and to the Holy Spirit' (the first line of the 'Minor Doxology', a short hymn which has been in liturgical use since at least the seventh century), are perhaps the most crucial affirmations of the Christian faith. Together what they mean is that the uncreated divine nature, which we glorify in giving glory to the divine persons of the Trinity, becomes wedded to our nature in the incarnation. The union of fallen human nature with the utterly holy divine nature necessarily changes the unholy: divine nature acts like a refining fire, burnishing away the tarnish of sin and death – and everything changes for us and for the whole cosmos as a result of this blessed marriage of the uncreated with the most cherished of all creatures.

Our salvation is worked precisely not by a work: it is not in the first instance what Christ does that saves us, but who he is: what he does is simply the logical working out of his identity as fully divine and fully human. That is perhaps why there are no heresies condemning any of the various theories of Christ's work or what he did; the Christological heresies are all concerned with Christ's person, with the question of who, exactly, he is. At the heart of the Christian belief lies this affirmation, that it is the sheer joining of divinity and humanity in a single person, Jesus Christ, which renovates the nature sickened by the Fall, yet this wondrous union not only heals our nature, but makes it better than it ever was before. The incarnation does not take us back to what we were in the garden of Eden. We were originally made, as Psalm 8 tells us, just a little lower than the angels, but through the incarnation, human nature receives blessings far beyond what is given to the angels. Through our union with Christ in baptism we are granted, each of us, the consequences of the union of divinity and humanity in Christ and are granted a relation to the blessed Trinity we could never otherwise have had: a relation of union.

This may seem radical, but the Church's belief is radical: it's more shocking and dangerous than anything dreamt up by what we call heretics. This conviction that Christ renovates us just by being who he is, both divine and human, is intimated in what Paul says in Romans 5: grace, righteousness and eternal life come to us through one man, Jesus Christ, and that phrase 'one man' echoes through the fifth chapter of Romans like a refrain. It is the conviction voiced also in Galatians 4.1–7 (quoted at the head of this chapter) when Paul says that God sent forth his son, born of a woman, that we might receive adoption as children of God: as the divine Word, the only Son of the eternal Father, took on our nature, he bound us to his Father, so we might be received into the divine family of the Trinity, as if we belonged there naturally. The eighty-fifth psalm announces that God's salvation is very near us, and the Gospel of Jesus Christ spells out for us just what this nearness means: it is like the nearness of a child in the womb to its mother, a nearness that makes Christ our brother and Mary the mother of us all, and which sends forth the Spirit into our hearts, calling 'Abba, Father' to the Master of the universe.

So we come back to where we started, to Nestorius's well-intentioned battles over a strange title for a woman of whom the Gospels give us only passing glimpses. One of the longest looks the Bible ever gives us of Mary is in the passage in Luke recounting the annunciation. Gabriel brings his startling news to this young girl, no doubt preoccupied with thoughts of her upcoming wedding, and surprisingly, she responds, 'Behold,

I am the handmaid of the Lord; let it be to me according to your word' (Luke 1.38). And in that moment, in that single moment, everything changes, a revolution of the entire cosmos as the result of a girl's 'yes' to God. For in Christian belief, from this first moment of the union of divinity and humanity in the Word newly conceived in a woman's womb, our nature is taken back to its newly minted state as when it was first created and instantly stretches beyond that, to what Adam and Eve could never have been, the adopted children of God. In that moment, the wound of the Fall, which like a vast gash ripped apart the harmony of the universe, is healed. In that moment, the whole world is turned back towards its creator and set on the path towards the final reconciliation: a reconciliation in which righteousness and peace will kiss each other, the lion will lie down with the lamb, the swords of human hatred will be beaten into ploughshares of peace, and all created things, in whatever voice they have, will join with the angels and the archangels and all the glorious company of heaven, singing (in the words of the 'Sanctus', the liturgical hymn based on Isaiah 6.3): 'Holy, holy, holy, Lord God of hosts, heaven and earth are full of your glory! Glory be to you, O Lord most high!'

All of it was wrought in that moment – that is what Nestorius never understood. It took nothing more than this tender dwelling of the Word with us, uniting God and humanity in himself. By that moment, and in that moment, all things were made new. Thanks be to God!

4

Eutychianism:
Is Jesus Christ divine and human
or a hybrid, a third thing that is
neither fully one nor the other?

MARCUS PLESTED

What is Eutychianism?

Eutychianism is the heresy which denies that there are two natures in Christ. It is named after Eutyches, the monastic superior of a large monastery at Constantinople, who was born in about 378 and died in 454. He held that there was only one nature (*physis*) in Christ 'after the union' of his divinity and humanity, and for this reason his view is sometimes called Monophysitism. Eutyches taught that Christ's humanity was so united with his divinity that it was not the same as ours, a view which the Fourth Ecumenical Council, held at Chalcedon in 451, decreed to be incompatible with our salvation through him.

* * *

Key Scriptures

He left Judea and departed again to Galilee. He had to pass through Samaria. So he came to a city of Samaria, called Sychar, near the field that Jacob gave to his son Joseph. Jacob's well was there, and so Jesus, wearied as he was with his journey, sat down beside the well. It was about the sixth hour.

There came a woman of Samaria to draw water. Jesus said to her, 'Give me a drink.' For his disciples had gone away into the city to buy food. The Samaritan woman said to him, 'How is it that you, a Jew, ask a drink of me, a woman of Samaria?' For Jews have no dealing with Samaritans. Jesus answered her, 'If you knew the gift of God, and who it is that is saying to you, "Give me a drink," you would have asked him, and he would have given you living water.' (John 4.3–10)

Since then we have a great high priest who has passed through the heavens, Jesus, the Son of God, let us hold fast our confession. For we have not a high priest who is unable to sympathize with our weaknesses, but one who in every respect has been tempted as we are, yet without sinning. Let us then with confidence draw near to the throne of grace, that we may receive mercy and find grace to help in time of need. (Hebrews 4.14–16)

*   *   *

Heresy can be a good thing. It is natural for the human mind to ask questions, to ask 'Why?' and if no one had ever questioned, for example, Christ's perfect divinity, the doctrine of the Holy Trinity would never have been affirmed so categorically. Likewise, if no one had ever questioned Christ's perfect humanity, that too might have remained a grey area. Heresy, in other words, is often the prompter of orthodoxy. This is not to say that orthodoxy, 'correct thinking', is simply a reaction to wrong thinking. Orthodoxy, rather, is the articulation of the apostolic faith within the tradition of the living and worshipping Church. It is the expression of what the Church already knows, even if it takes a new question to bring that knowledge into the light.

'Heresy' according to its Greek root denotes 'opinion' or 'school of thought'. Paul in his first letter to the Corinthians writes that it's well there should be different opinions (literally, 'heresies') among them 'in order that those who are genuine may be recognized' (1 Corinthians 11.19). It was only later that the term acquired its pejorative meaning of 'erroneous opinion' or a school of thought defined by its opposition to established Church teaching.

However, we must always remember that heresy is a category imposed by the victors. Those castigated as heretics did not, by and large, set out to propagate teachings contrary to established church teaching. They sought rather to raise important and legitimate questions as to the very substance of the faith. In the great controversies of the fourth and fifth centuries concerning the Trinity and the person of Christ, all was to play for. None of the protagonists claimed to be doing anything but witnessing faithfully to the Christ of the Scriptures and to be acting within the authentic church tradition. That said, there is a great difference between truth claims and truth – or at least truth so far as this can be apprehended by human beings. We can never be entirely right in what we say about God, but we can certainly very easily be wrong. The concept of heresy remains essential for distinguishing between an incorrect and a correct (or at least less incorrect) articulation of the faith.

One such incorrect articulation is the heresy of Eutychianism. This is far from being a common temptation these days but it does represent a way of thinking that has potentially disastrous implications for our understanding of Christ and the salvation wrought by him. Put in a nutshell, Eutychianism is the view that the union between God and humanity in Christ is so complete that his humanity is no longer distinguishable from his divinity. We must, therefore, speak of one and only one nature in Christ. Christ's humanity is not of the same nature as ours: in effect it has been subsumed in the divinity. Thus a third thing, a *tertium quid*, has come into being – neither God nor man, but God-man.

The construction and detection of heresy is always to some extent an artificial enterprise and it should be noted that virtually no one has ever actually taught this heresy and that Eutyches himself was in all probability not a Eutychian. To understand this apparent anomaly we must, as always, look at the historical context in which the heresy first emerged.

Eutyches was a powerful and influential archimandrite or monastic superior resident in the imperial city of Constantinople. He had taken grave exception to Nestorius and to the separation between Christ's divinity and humanity that he detected in Nestorius's teaching (see Chapter 3). However, just as Nestorius's problem was an inadequate account of the union in Christ (he used the same term *prosopon*, meaning something like 'face' or 'person', both for what was two in Christ and for what was one), so Eutyches had an inadequate grasp of the distinction between God and man in Christ. For him even the merest mention of any form of two-ness in Christ meant dualism, separation, two Christs – in short, Nestorianism. Eutyches consequently insisted on speaking of only one reality, one nature in Christ.

In speaking of only one nature, Eutyches believed that he was remaining loyal to the teaching of Cyril of Alexandria, the formidable archbishop of Alexandria who had secured the condemnation of Nestorius at the Ecumenical Council of Ephesus in 431. By this victory, Cyril had established himself as the touchstone of Christological orthodoxy to such an extent that almost all subsequent Christological debate revolved around the question of fidelity to Cyril. Cyril had been particularly fond of the slogan 'one incarnate nature of God the Word incarnate', a slogan he believed derived from the impeccably orthodox Athanasius of Alexandria, but in fact came (unbeknown to all at the time) from the heretical Apollinarius, who had taught that the Word had taken the place of the rational human soul in Christ (as discussed in Chapter 2). For Cyril, however, 'one nature' language was a way of guarding and proclaiming the fundamental unity of Christ. It did not rule out recognition of Christ's full and distinct human nature. Cyril, especially in the years following Ephesus, had been very clear on this last point. He affirmed Christ's full humanity – possessed of a rational soul and born of the Virgin – and declared that this human nature was in no way confused with or subsumed into the divinity. He allowed that one could speak in terms of 'two natures' so long as this did not detract in any way from the perfection of the union.

Eutyches appears to have lacked any real appreciation of the range and subtlety of Cyril's thinking. For Eutyches, it was simply a case of 'one nature good; two natures bad'. He was not an Apollinarian – and indeed explicitly affirmed Christ's perfect humanity – but he had no way of accounting for the ongoing distinction between God and man in Christ. When brought before the standing council or 'home synod' of Constantinople in 448, Eutyches admitted that Christ might be spoken of as two natures before the union, but only one nature 'after the union'. He was also most reluctant to affirm that Christ's body was of the same nature as, or consubstantial with, our own. Perfectly reasonably, he argued that such language was not found either in Scripture or in the Fathers. He was, however, prepared to concede this point – under very heavy pressure – as a sign of his respect for episcopal authority. This concession was not enough for the assembled bishops and Eutyches was condemned for his insistence on one nature – and only one nature – in Christ.

4. Eutyches' reluctance to allow that Christ is consubstantial with us was very probably a result of his very high eucharistic theology: for him the body and blood were the body and blood of God. To claim otherwise would be to empty them of their life-giving qualities. Eutyches' view on this issue has generally been taken to imply that he believed Christ's body in the Eucharist has been changed or absorbed into his divinity. Of course, Eutyches did not say this outright, but the fact that he could tremble on the brink of saying it may be attributable to a deep-seated suspicion that the expression 'consubstantial

with us' might lend itself to a Nestorian interpretation, separating the man from the Word and thus depriving the Eucharist of its efficacy. That he had so obviously inadequate a grasp of the distinction between divinity and humanity in Christ does give a certain weight to his connection with the eponymous heresy.

Eutyches' fortunes suffered something of a roller-coaster ride in the years following his appearance before the home synod. These ups and downs ended in a city called Chalcedon, opposite Constantinople on the Bosphorus, where in 451 an Ecumenical Council was convoked by the Emperor Marcian. Here it was that Eutyches' teaching was finally condemned in what became known as 'the Chalcedonian Definition' (see pp. 11–12).

Chalcedon represents a brilliant theological synthesis of the various approaches to the mystery of the person of Christ. The council affirmed both unity and distinction in Christ, his two natures concurring in 'one person and one existence (*hypostasis*)'. In a fabulous sequence of negative affirmations, a veritable masterpiece of apophatic theology (that is, theology defined by negations), Chalcedon proclaimed that perfect divinity and perfect humanity are united in Christ 'without confusion, without change, without division, without separation'. 'Without confusion' and 'without change' rule out Eutychianism while 'without division' and 'without separation' rule out Nestorianism.

Brilliant as it was, Chalcedon was perhaps rather too subtle for its own good. The simple fact that it spoke of 'two natures', however qualified, was enough to raise suspicions of Nestorianism. A number of bishops at the Council admitted frankly that they would be lynched if they went back to their flocks with anything but a one-nature formulation, the confession of one nature being widely seen as a badge of allegiance to the memory and teaching of the great Cyril. Indeed, as it transpired, Chalcedon's apparent betrayal of Cyril led to what remains an ongoing schism (a formal separation) between the western churches and the Oriental Orthodox churches (Coptic, Armenian, Syrian, and Indian Orthodox). The Oriental churches prefer some form of 'one nature' confession, albeit one which recognizes Christ's perfect humanity and the ongoing distinction between that humanity and his divinity. All these churches condemn both Eutyches and Eutychianism but, most unfortunately, they have been routinely disparaged as Eutychian down through the ages. This unwarranted association is latent in the common term 'Monophysite' ('one *and only one* nature-ites') frequently used for these churches, but it is more just to refer to them not as 'Monophysites' but 'Miaphysite' ('*primarily* one nature-ites').

But how does all this matter to anyone who is not a professional theologian or ecumenist? Why should we be worried about avoiding Eutychianism? What, in short, is wrong with it?

First and foremost, we must recognize the fact that to deny the real distinction between God and man in Christ is to imperil our salvation. It is an axiom of patristic theology that only God can save but that only man needs to be saved. The Saviour must, therefore, be both God and man if salvation is to be effected. Eutychianism removes the authentically human dimension of Christ's saving work. It makes salvation into a mere fiat, a divine action disconnected from God's free human creation. If Christ does not share our humanity, if he is not consubstantial with us, it becomes very difficult to understand how his salvation could be extended to the whole human race. As the scriptural passages quoted at the head of this chapter show, he was indeed consubstantial with us: divine, yes (able to supply 'living water' and sinless), but human too (susceptible to weariness and thirst and subject to temptation). In a Eutychian scenario the incarnation would have no significance beyond the experience of the hybrid God-man himself.

Second, Eutychianism raises problems for our understanding of the Eucharist. As I have said, Eutyches regarded the eucharistic elements as the very body and blood of God. This is, of course, true within a traditional Orthodox or Roman Catholic perspective, so long as one understands that they are the body and blood of the Son of God incarnate. Eutychian eucharistic theology would presumably make un-adulterated theophages (God-eaters) of us all. This in turn exposes a more general flaw in Eutychianism: a failure to make sufficient allowance for the distinctiveness of three persons of the consubstantial Trinity.

We must also consider that if Christ's humanity was absorbed into his divinity, there can be no prospect of our humanity surviving intact in any form of encounter with God. The Orthodox Christian tradition tends to speak of salvation in terms of a deifying union between God and the human being, a union through which the human being becomes divine by grace, while remaining created by nature. A Eutychian Christ would effectively abolish the ontological gap between created and uncreated natures, making such a process of deification (*theosis*) impossible. All we could hope for would be a process whereby we are subsumed into God. To all intents and purposes, we would cease to exist. Eutychianism, in other words, abolishes our eternal and unique characteristics as human beings.

If there is indeed no eternal future for the human being, Eutychian salvation is of little more value than some sort of return to the void from whence we came or the illusory 'resurrection' offered by Philip Pullman's child heroes to the shades of the dead in his novel, *The Amber Spyglass*. In this story, the dead are offered a chance to be resolved into the elements, to 'turn into the night, the starlight, the air . . .' They vanish, 'leaving behind such a vivid little burst of happiness [like] the bubbles in a glass of champagne'. While this is an arresting and even, superficially, a beautiful image, it does not obscure the fact that this is the end. Death is all there is. And death makes life pointless and absurd. While coming from entirely different perspectives, Eutyches and Pullman alike deny the eternal significance and potential of the human being.

Having singled out the main problems of Eutychianism, how are we to avoid it? I think it must be evident that this is not a widespread heresy, and not one into which many contemporary Christians are likely to fall, although, as discussed in Chapter 6, the growing tendency among modern theologians to say that Christ suffered in his divine nature is a kind of Eutychian error, changing divine immutability into, or confusing it with, human passibility. But whether Eutychianism today is common or rare, we can avoid it by resisting any account of salvation that is not the work of the one who is both fully God and fully man. Likewise, we will avoid it if we remember constantly the eternal value, uniqueness, and integrity of each and every human being. Perhaps most importantly, we can avoid Eutychianism if we pray for and seek out the deifying union without confusion by which we are incorporated into the Trinitarian life of the Godhead while remaining eternally distinct by nature. As Macarius-Symeon, the late fourth-century author of the *Macarian Homilies*, put it:

> [At the resurrection] all the members become translucent, all are plunged into light and fire, and transformed; they are not, as some say, destroyed, they do not become fire, their own nature ceasing to subsist. For Peter remains Peter, and Paul remains Paul, and Philip remains Philip. Each retains his own nature and hypostasis, filled by the Spirit. (*Homilies* 15.10)

We may be deified, but we are not thereby lost in the Godhead. In this we follow the example of Jesus, in whom humanity is united with divinity – without confusion, without change, without division, and without separation.

5

Adoptionism:
Is Jesus Christ the Son of
God by nature or by adoption?

RACHEL MUERS

* * *

What is Adoptionism?

Adoptionism is the heresy which asserts a double sonship in Jesus Christ: as divine, Christ is the Son of God by generation and nature, but as human he is the Son of God by adoption and grace. By separating the divinity and humanity of Christ in this way, it can be considered an off-shoot of Nestorianism (for more on which, see Chapter 3). It originated in Spain in the eighth century and is chiefly associated with the archbishop of Toledo, Elipandus (717–802). It was condemned in a letter to the bishops of Spain by Pope Hadrian I in 785, and by the Council of Frankfurt in 794.

*   *   *

Key Scriptures

Listen to me, O coastlands, and hearken, you peoples from afar. The LORD called me from the womb, from the body of my mother he named my name. He made my mouth like a sharp sword, in the shadow of his hand he hid me; he made me a polished arrow, in his quiver he hid me away. And he said to me, 'You are my servant, Israel, in whom I will be glorified.' But I said, 'I have laboured in vain, I have spent my strength for nothing and vanity; yet surely my right is with the LORD, and my recompense with my God.'

And now the LORD says, who formed me from the womb to be his servant, to bring Jacob back to him, and that Israel might be gathered to him, for I am honoured in the eyes of the LORD, and my God has become my strength – he says: 'It is too light a thing that you should be my servant to raise up the tribes of Jacob and to restore the preserved of Israel; I will give you as a light to the nations, that my salvation may reach to the end of the earth.'

Thus says the LORD, the Redeemer of Israel and his Holy One, to one deeply despised, abhorred by the nations, the servant of rulers: 'Kings shall see and arise; princes, and they shall prostrate themselves; because of the LORD, who is faithful, the Holy One of Israel, who has chosen you.' (Isaiah 49.1–7)

As the people were in expectation, and all men questioned in their hearts concerning John, whether perhaps he were the Christ, John answered them all, 'I baptize with water; but he who is mightier than I is coming, the thong of whose sandals I am not worthy to untie; he will baptize you with the Holy Spirit and with fire. His winnowing fork is in his hand, to clear his threshing floor, and to gather the wheat into his granary, but the chaff he will burn with unquenchable fire.'

. . . Now when all the people were baptized, and when Jesus also had been baptized and was praying, the heaven was opened, and the Holy Spirit descended upon him in bodily form, as a dove, and a voice came from heaven, 'Thou art my beloved Son; with thee I am well pleased.' (Luke 3.15–17, 21–22)

*   *   *

If you look in accounts of the history of doctrine for a quick definition of Adoptionism, you will read that it is the belief that the human being Jesus of Nazareth is the Son of God not by nature but by adoption. You might see it linked specifically to the baptism story in Luke 3 (quoted above) and to the idea that Jesus of Nazareth became the Son of God at this moment, the moment of his baptism.

Any attempt to explore more about what this means will take you very quickly into the thickets of centuries of debate about exactly what can be said about the divinity and the humanity of Jesus Christ, and it will take you in different directions depending on which version of Adoptionism the writer has decided to focus on. Historical accounts of Adoptionism contain references to a very wide range of people, times and places. That is perhaps important in itself, because it serves as a reminder that heresies, or the issues they represent, keep coming back. In its most prominent form, the one I want to discuss here, it was advocated by a group of (mostly) Spanish theologians, notably Elipandus – hardly a household name, even among historians of Christian doctrine – and condemned by Pope Hadrian I, in the eighth century.

So what is actually wrong with Adoptionism, with this central claim that Jesus of Nazareth is the Son of God by adoption? First, we need to be clear about what Adoptionists are not saying. They do not want to deny the Trinity, nor to deny that God the Son is eternally God. What they are trying to work out is how we can and cannot speak about the human being who was born in Bethlehem, baptized in the Jordan by John the Baptist, and executed not very long afterwards by the Roman authorities. And here again, their heresy is not the obvious one. They do not want to deny that Jesus Christ is fully divine as well as fully human. The issue is what it really means to call the human being Jesus of Nazareth 'Son of God'.

Now, as a way into what Adoptionists are in fact saying, I want to suggest that there are a lot of wrong ways to avoid Adoptionism, and that many of them are more wrong than Adoptionism itself. Let's start with our text from Luke. Some early versions of Adoptionism, as I have said (but not the eighth-century Spanish theologians, who were a good deal more sophisticated) picked out this event, Jesus's baptism, as the point at which the man, Jesus of Nazareth, became the Son of God. And notice that in this text Jesus, in coming to be baptized, stands with 'all the people'. He goes the same route that 'all the people' go. He does not stand out from the crowd, rather he is just one of the crowd. And the descent of the Holy Spirit 'in bodily form' looks, if you're joining the story at this point and haven't read the first two-and-a-half chapters of Luke, like the magic finger in a lottery advertisement a few years ago that descended from the sky to pick out the lucky winner while a voice-over said: 'It could be you' (or, by implication, absolutely anyone else). In fact, in this text John the Baptist is the man who looks more than human – which is why he's the one about whom people are asking questions.

So Adoptionism here seems to be doing something right, something this text calls its readers to do, in being suspicious of saying that Jesus's way of being human was 'special' – in keeping Jesus's feet firmly planted on the ground. And we can see from this what might be a 'wrong' way to avoid Adoptionism. We might have assumed that the best way to avoid Adoptionism is to make Jesus less like us, to emphasize the uniqueness of Jesus – or, more precisely, to say that what it meant for Jesus to be human is fundamentally different from what it means for you or me to be human. But it is easy to see that this could end up making Jesus not really human; and in talking about Jesus, as debates around other heresies have made clear, 'not really human' is always 'less than human', never 'more than human'. Whatever moves we make in avoiding Adoptionism, it's important never to deny Jesus his place among 'all the people'.

In fact Elipandus, when he asserted that Jesus of Nazareth was Son of God 'adoptively', was trying to convey a very important insight about Jesus's baptism and what it represents. He wanted to say that just as God lifts up Jesus of Nazareth – from this moment of affirming him as 'beloved son' through to his resurrection and ascension – God lifts up all of us who are Jesus's brothers and sisters. The journey towards sharing in God's glory that this man Jesus of Nazareth makes is the journey that we all come to make. We share in his glorification, we each become someone to whom God says, 'You are my beloved child, with you I am well pleased.' So if we are 'adopted' as God's children, Elipandus said – if that is a good way to talk about our relationship to God in Christ, about the gift we receive in Christ – it must also be a possible way to talk about the relationship to God of the man Jesus.

Elipandus also argued that to talk about Jesus's sonship as 'adoptive' was the best way to do justice to the humiliation of the Son of God in Jesus of Nazareth, the best way to say that, as we read in Philippians 2.6, the Son of God 'did not count equality with God a thing to be grasped'. The Son of God gives up, in the incarnation, his rights as a son 'by nature', and goes the way of humiliation and exaltation to receive his sonship 'by adoption'.

Incidentally, most heresies discussed in this book seem, as I read them, to be the result of somebody trying to make things too tidy, refusing to take theological risks. Adoptionism as I've just described it is, if anything, the opposite. The later Adoptionists, if not the earlier ones, knew they were taking a risk in describing Jesus of Nazareth as Son of God 'by adoption', and they knew it might make a mess of other bits of the Christological picture. They did it because they wanted to emphasize to the point of hyperbole the idea that everything God gives to Jesus of Nazareth, God gives to us; and also the idea of the complete 'giving up' of the status proper to God that the incarnation represents. They were pushing the language used to speak about Jesus's co-humanity with the rest of humanity as far as it would go.

Another way to think about this might be to consider what it means to be an adoptive child or an adoptive parent, as we normally understand it. Numerous adoptive parents and adoptive children will testify, I think, that adoption puts up no barriers to saying 'you are my beloved child'. The fact of adoption doesn't say anything about the quality of the relationship or the status of the child in the family. That is what the

Adoptionists get absolutely right. Your adoptive children are your children. As adoptive children of God we don't have to settle for second best; we really are heirs to God's kingdom, full sharers in the love of God.

In fact, we might be able to say, not just that your adoptive children are your children, but that your children are always 'adoptive'. When my son was born, among my earliest reactions when I saw him were surprise and confusion. That was partly because when you've just given birth you aren't thinking quite straight, and partly because newborn babies don't look anything like the babies in advertisements, but more fundamentally, I think, because I was meeting a stranger. It would take time – not long, but some time – before I could meaningfully echo the words from Luke, 'Thou art my beloved Son; with thee I am well pleased' (Luke 3.22). (I've heard the Luke text very differently since I realized it is exactly the sort of thing I say to my son all the time, while he's still young enough for it not to embarrass him: 'You're my beautiful baby, I love you.') So although he was mine by nature, he also became mine. In a sense I had to adopt him as mine. Adoptionists are trying to capture something like that in what they say about the relationship between God and the man, Jesus of Nazareth – that Jesus's identity as Son of God is bound up with his story, it happens over time. Events in his life, like the baptism, are integral to what it means for this man, living his life among 'all the people', to be Son of God.

But I suspect that's exactly where the dangers come in, and where we find our reasons to avoid Adoptionism. My son was my son anyway – even when I was looking at his strange alien-like newborn face and wondering how it was possible to relate to this person. From the moment he came into existence, I was a parent; and I could be a good parent or a bad parent or even an absent parent, but I wouldn't be able *not* to be a parent again. His existence changed who I was. I was irrevocably committed to him regardless of what he chose to do or what I chose to do. The process of learning to live as his mother was actually a process of learning to be what I already was, whether I liked it or not (I did).

And reflecting on this, I think the reason to avoid Adoptionism is perhaps not in the first place to do with what we want to say about Jesus of Nazareth and his status – as if an adopted child were any less a beloved child, any less a sharer in the parent's life – but more to do with what we want to say about God. Saying that Jesus of Nazareth is Son of God from his beginning – by nature – is proclaiming God's irrevocable commitment to a human life, from beginning to end; and thus it's proclaiming God's irrevocable commitment to *everything* human beings are by their creation. What Adoptionism risks missing, I think, is that what happens to Jesus of Nazareth and in Jesus of Nazareth isn't just (or isn't mainly) about him or any other human being becoming a child of God; it's about God becoming a parent of humanity, through this particular human life.

And this, of course, also ends up being a claim about Jesus of Nazareth. No particular characteristic, no particular event, no particular action, makes him Son of God. God never 'zaps in' to his life, his relationship to God isn't an added extra that could be seen, specified, quantified or even really imitated. His entire life is the word of God to the world, is God's gift of God's self to the world. As in Isaiah 49.1–7, quoted at the head of this chapter, the one who is called 'from the womb' is the one who is 'a light to the nations', the mediator of the blessings of God. The Isaiah text suggests that the servant of God can do this, despite being hidden and despite being an apparent failure, just because he has never not been a servant. His servanthood is about *who* he is, not what he is; there is nothing about his life, from beginning to end, that is not included in his servanthood.

So to avoid Adoptionism we have to find ways of saying that Jesus's life, death and resurrection isn't just an example, or even the first example, of the sort of thing that happens to the children of God; it's the life, death and resurrection through which God makes it possible for there to be people who are called 'children of God'. The word from God at Jesus's baptism, then, doesn't just say, 'It could be you, too' to all those people who are standing with Jesus; it says, 'Because this person exists, it will be you, too.' We don't become children of God separately; we become children of God in relation to the firstborn son of God. We join a particular family.

Perhaps strangely, naming Jesus as Son of God by nature makes it easier, not harder, to understand ourselves as children of God by adoption, because, if this is the case, all that's needed in order to be children of God is to stand with Jesus of Nazareth. We can go back to the baptism scene by the Jordan and hear Jesus named as the beloved Son *on behalf of* 'all the people' among whom he stands. They now don't have to wait to be plucked out of the crowd; they don't have to work out what's so special about this particular man, and try to emulate that. They have just received, if they could recognize it, their welcome into the family of God. You can look to Jesus to find out what it means to be a child of God; but what you will find out is that being a child of God means simply being who you are, and accepting the love of God for everything that you are.

What's the importance today of a call to avoid Adoptionism? Avoiding Adoptionism means speaking more about Jesus's singularity, focusing on a single body (from birth to death) as the place where the life of God is given to be the life of the world. That is, it seems to me, difficult in a context in which we are encouraged in many ways to think of an individual person, or a person's individuality, as a bundle of personal data, transferable skills, measurable characteristics. Christianity sometimes works that way as well, however hard we try to avoid it. In wider public perception, your religion becomes 'another thing you do', another fact among other facts about you; in Christians' perceptions, Christianity becomes associated with (can we admit this?) a set of expected patterns of behaviour and appearance, a way of 'being good'. It's difficult to hold to the claim that being a child of God is not like that; that it's a relationship of God to the whole person and the whole person to God. We can be helped in that affirmation by reading these texts – by hearing the servant of God affirmed as such even when he's at his most obscure, hidden in the womb, hidden in consciousness of his own failure; and then by hearing the beloved son of God affirmed when he's doing nothing special, merely standing with all the people.

So, in conclusion, I think it's important to recognize the strength of Adoptionism: it's important not to be afraid – as the Adoptionists were not afraid – to take risks in our speech about God; it's important to affirm that we share in the journey Jesus of Nazareth makes, and he in the journey we make. And then it's important to challenge anything that might deny to us what Paul called the 'glorious liberty of the children of God' (Romans 8.21), that might make us anxious about whether we really belong to God's family, and that would take away the assurance that the love of God spoken in, as well as to, Jesus of Nazareth, should give us.

6

Theopaschitism: Is Jesus Christ able or unable to suffer in his divine nature?

MICHAEL WARD

❖❖❖

What is Theopaschitism?

Theopaschitism is the heresy which asserts that the union of divinity and humanity in Jesus Christ means that it is possible for the divine nature to suffer. It arose in the fifth century and is associated chiefly with Peter the Fuller, patriarch of Antioch, a Monophysite (see Chapter 4), who died in 488, and with John Maxentius, a Scythian monk, who in 519 defended the formula 'one of the Trinity suffered in the flesh'. The teaching was rejected by the patriarch of Constantinople and by Hormisdas, bishop of Rome (died 523).

*   *   *

Key Scriptures

'I the LORD do not change.' (Malachi 3.6)

Then Pilate took Jesus and scourged him. And the soldiers plaited a crown of thorns, and put it on his head, and arrayed him in a purple robe; they came up to him, saying, 'Hail, King of the Jews!' and struck him with their hands. Pilate went out again, and said to them, 'Behold, I am bringing him out to you, that you may know that I find no crime in him.' So Jesus came out, wearing the crown of thorns and the purple robe. Pilate said to them, 'Here is the man!' When the chief priests and the officers saw him, they cried out, 'Crucify him, crucify him!' Pilate said to them, 'Take him yourselves and crucify him, for I find no crime in him.' The Jews answered him, 'We have a law, and by that law he ought to die, because he has made himself the Son of God.' When Pilate heard these words, he was the more afraid; he entered the praetorium again and said to Jesus, 'Where are you from?' But Jesus gave no answer. Pilate therefore said to him, 'You will not speak to me? Do you not know that I have power to release you, and power to crucify you?' Jesus answered him, 'You would have no power over me unless it had been given you from above.' (John 19.1–11a)

* * *

Heresy, as we have seen, comes from the Greek word for 'choice'. In the first four chapters of this book we've been reminded of the four 'choices' which eventually provoked the Chalcedonian Definition in 451: the heresies of Arianism, Docetism, Nestorianism and Eutychianism. As we've investigated the history of these four debates we've found that the alternative to orthodoxy was always quite plausible, quite attractive and convincing; it took intellectual effort, moral courage and political skill to resist it. Chesterton sums up the matter well in his book *Orthodoxy*:

> It is easy to be a heretic. It is always easy to let the age have its head; the difficult thing is to keep one's own . . . It is always simple to fall; there are an infinity of angles at which one falls, only one at which one stands. To have fallen into any one of the fads [of the heretics] would indeed have been obvious and tame. But to avoid them all has been one whirling adventure; and in my vision the heavenly chariot [of the Church] flies thundering through the ages, the dull heresies sprawling and prostrate, the wild truth reeling but erect. (G. K. Chesterton, *Orthodoxy*, chapter 6)

The dull heresies, alas, do not go away. They are always lurking in the undergrowth, ready to suck us into their dullness. Several centuries after Nestorianism had been condemned, it reappeared in the form of Adoptionism, a fresh attempt to separate and divide Christ's humanity and divinity (see Chapter 5). And just as Nestorianism didn't lie down and die, neither did Eutychianism. A fresh attempt to confuse and change Christ's humanity and divinity occurred in the heresy of Theopaschitism, which is the belief that, by virtue of the inseparable and indivisible unity of Christ's divine and human natures, it may properly be said that God suffered as God when Christ was crucified. This was a belief held in the fifth and sixth centuries, and is associated chiefly with the figures of Peter the Fuller, patriarch of Antioch, and John Maxentius, a Scythian monk, and it's a belief very widely held among theologians today. In fact, so widespread has this belief become over the course of the last hundred years or so that it's been described as the new orthodoxy. My aim, in the next few pages, is to give an account of why the subject has again become a live issue and to show why we should want to avoid it. I will attempt, with a brevity which is as risky as it is necessary, to restate the traditional position that God is impassible. By 'impassible' I mean basically that God can't be changed from without and that he can't change himself from within, specifically that he can't change or be changed from a better to a worse state, that change we call suffering.

A thumbnail sketch of the large-scale abandonment of belief in God's impassibility during the last century or so would include many things, but let's just mention three. The first two we'll consider very briefly, the third we'll look at in more detail.

So, first, our sketch of the rise of modern Theopaschitism would include: new strains of historical theology, particularly that movement known as 'the history of dogma', which argues that the early Church's doctrines were influenced by ideas from Greek philosophy. To Plato and Aristotle and others the divine nature was obviously impassible, and the early Church, through Hellenistic Jews such as Philo, allowed itself to be unduly affected by these ideas.

In response we can say that all ideas are influenced by the cultures in which they arise, and that the ideas of Theopaschitism are no more immune to such influence than the ideas of the impassibilists. If the impassibilists were influenced by Greek philosophy, well, weren't the modern Theopaschites influenced by contemporary philosophy, such as the 'process thought' of Alfred North Whitehead and others? But this just levels the playing-field; it doesn't get us anywhere. What is more relevant to point out is that the early Christian doctrine of impassibility was partly shaped *in distinction from* some contemporary pagan philosophical propositions. Strains of Stoicism and Gnosticism argued that God, along with the whole universe, would dissolve at the end of time, a belief which showed God to be subject to cosmic processes. Two early church leaders, Justin and Irenaeus, held out against Stoicism and Gnosticism respectively. If God were the transcendent Creator, to group him with created things or to suggest that he was constrained by them would self-evidently be incorrect. In advocating divine impassibility, the early Church demonstrated critical engagement with their contemporaries' philosophy and resisted certain ideas which didn't seem to accord with the Christian account. The doctrine of impassibility, although partly compatible with certain pagan ideas, wasn't uncritically in accord with them either.

Second, in our sketch of the rise of modern Theopaschitism, we may note certain new strains of biblical criticism, which have drawn fresh attention to the Bible's depiction of God as intimately and emotionally involved with the fate of the people of Israel, alternately grieved and gladdened by their behaviour. The stormily emotional God of the Old Testament does not, it is maintained, sit well with the notion of a God who cannot change or be changed.

In response to this we can agree that God is shown as emotionally involved with his people, but need to point out that the Bible also shows immutability in the divine nature: for instance, 'God is not a man, that he should lie, or a son of man, that he should repent [i.e., change his mind]' (Numbers 23.19); 'I the Lord do not change' (Malachi 3.6); with God 'there is no variation or shadow due to change' (James 1.17); 'Jesus Christ is the same yesterday and today and for ever' (Hebrews 13.8); 'if we are faithless, he remains faithful – for he cannot deny himself' (2 Timothy 2.13). In order to interpret the full range of scriptural testimony, theologians such as Anselm and Aquinas argued that God's unchangeableness was our starting-point and that God's emotional involvement was therefore to be understood figuratively or relatively. If Anselm and Aquinas had known about Copernicus they might well have pointed out that, just as the sun seems to us to move across the sky, while in reality it is the earth that is moving, so God's emotional changeability is an effect of human perspective.

Third, and most important, in our sketch of the rise of modern Theopaschitism, we would have to include the impact of the two world wars in the first half of the last century, for how could anyone believe in a God who was above and beyond the terrible suffering brought about by mechanized warfare? How could an impassible God have anything to say to the people of Hiroshima or to the Jews of the death camps? A particular touchstone is Elie Wiesel's horrific story of the hanging in Auschwitz of a youth in front of the whole camp:

> The death throes of the youth lasted for half an hour. 'Where is God? Where is he?' someone asked behind me. As the youth still hung in torment in the noose after a long time, I heard the man call again, 'Where is God now?' And I heard a voice in myself answer: 'Where is he? He is here. He is hanging there on the gallows.' (Elie Wiesel, *Night*, p. 79)

The theologian Jürgen Moltmann, author of *The Crucified God*, who was himself a prisoner of war, wrote in support of Wiesel's story: 'Any other answer would be blasphemy. There cannot be any other Christian answer to the question of this torment. To speak here of a God who could not suffer would make God a demon.'

To Moltmann, the cross is not just where mankind is saved from sin; it is where God is saved from being a demon. By suffering in his divine nature God shows his love for us. An impassible God would be distant and aloof and unloving.

But why then for most of Christian history has God been thought to be impassible? Can we suppose that, for nearly nineteen hundred years, the Church was content to worship a God who was cold and distant and uninvolved? Can we claim that previous ages didn't know the full scale of human suffering? True, they didn't know the full horrors of industrialized warfare, but then neither did they know the benefits of chloroform or penicillin or any of those other major advances in medicine and technology that have done so much to change the average human life from being solitary, poor, nasty, brutish and short. The traditional picture of an impassible but yet still loving God can't have arisen simply because people weren't then aware of the depths of human suffering. It must have a good deal to recommend it, even if it's not on the face of it immediately easy to understand. And in the rest of this chapter I'm going to try to draw out two main features of the traditional picture and show why Theopaschitism is worth avoiding. In doing so, I'll be relying heavily on Thomas Weinandy's important and influential work, *Does God Suffer?*

And the first thing to say is to correct the impression I might just have given when I wrote of God being impassible 'but yet still loving'. That was the wrong way to put it. It leaves the impression that God's love and God's impassibility are two contrary things, which need somehow to be held in tension. But this is not so. God isn't loving *despite* being impassible: he is loving *because* he is impassible. Remember our definition: the impassible God can't be acted upon from without and can't change himself from within. If 'God is love', that's good news.

And God is love! This resounding statement from 1 John 4 has been traditionally understood to mean not just that God is loving towards his creation but that he is love in and of himself, even when considered entirely separately from us. God's nature is *essentially* loving because God is eternally and perfectly constituted by the loving relationships which obtain between the three persons of the Trinity.

These intra-Trinitarian relationships are different from human relationships because we human beings are only partly defined by our relationships. Take my own father, for instance. He is not completely defined by virtue of the fact that I'm his son: he is also the father of my two brothers; he is my mother's husband. And if I and my brothers and my mother were all suddenly killed, my father would continue to exist. He has an independent integrity apart from his relationships.

But the persons of the Trinity are eternally and completely constituted only in relation to one another. They subsist in these relationships and can't be understood as having a reality outside them. To pick up a point made in the chapter on Docetism (Chapter 2), we should think of the persons of the Trinity more as if they were verbs than as if they were nouns. God the Father isn't simply an individual who 'possesses' fatherhood as one attribute among many, like *my* father does. The term Father, when applied to God the Father, means more that he is 'fatherhood in action', he is eternally fathering the Son in the Spirit. There was never a time when there was only the Father; the Father and his Spirit of Sonship are eternal attributes of the divine nature. The Father, the Son and the Spirit are, so to speak, mutually dependent; they are reciprocally and eternally, albeit asymmetrically, related.

And since the Father, Son and Spirit subsist in their mutual relations, it follows that these relations, being fully and perfectly enacted, can't change or develop – not because they're static or inert or because they are somehow emotionally dead, but precisely for the opposite reason – they're so full of life. Because they are fully enacting their relational roles, the divine persons don't have any relational potential which would need to be actualized in order to make them more relational, more who they are. They are utterly and completely dynamic and active as Father, Son and Spirit. That is why we can say that God *is* love and need not say that God is merely *becoming* love. God 'cannot deny himself' and therefore he cannot become either less, or for that matter more, loving than he already is. He is impassible, he cannot change or be changed.

But because we are creatures of time and experience reality successively, we find this state of affairs hard to accept, both intellectually and – even more – at the level of our emotions. In human relationships a person who can't change or be changed is rarely thought to be attractive. We're likely to think them stony, remote, inhuman. But God's changelessness needs to be understood not as a monotonous or loveless fixity, but as a burning, inexhaustible, unwavering, loving determination. In the Eastern Orthodox tradition, God is said to possess 'apatheia', which does not mean apathy or insensitivity or indifference. Rather, it means that God has the freedom to act in a truly 'dispassionate' way, seeing clearly and acting voluntarily, unclouded by storms of passion, because nothing can divert his loving nature from being itself. Perhaps it would help to say that God is *dis*passionate, but not *un*passionate. His love is an action, not a reaction, and of course it includes what we would call passion (that is, 'strong feeling, emotion'), but it is not determined by 'emotion'; it is determined by his entire, steadfast, loving nature, of which 'emotion' is a part. A useful way to picture this may be to think of God's love as white light. White light by definition is colourless; but slow it down and refract it through a prism and you'll see vivid colours. If impassible love seems to us to be insipid or unattractive or over-controlled, we need to remember imaginatively that it is really constituted by the eternal loves constantly and perfectly exchanged within the Trinity, just as white light is all the colours of the rainbow, united. What from our creaturely perspective seems colourless, is actually colour at the maximum. Similarly, God's impassible love is love to the maximum. Well might we call it inhuman! It is not human, but divine: of uncreated, searing intensity, holy and unbearable. God dwells in unapproachable, unchangeable light, and in him there is no darkness at all.

Having reminded ourselves of God's holy and impassible love, we're now better placed to consider God's loving action in Christ towards our humanity. And surely here, in his dealings with the world, God must at last become passible; must become (in the words that W. H. Auden uses) 'weak and interesting' – weak and interesting like us. And yes, he does, provided that all proper weight is given to the words 'like us'. God can suffer like us, because we are human and we suffer. He cannot suffer like himself, for, as we have shown, he does not suffer in himself. To suffer is to change, and God does not change. How then can God suffer like us?

Here it will be useful to recall some of the other orthodoxies, those peculiarly upright positions, which we've discussed so far in this book. Christ is fully divine (which the Arians would deny) and fully human (which the Docetists would deny) and his two natures constitute one person (which the Nestorians would deny). And yet this one person is not simply a hybrid made up by squashing humanity and divinity together so that they make up a third thing which is neither fully the one nor the other, as the Eutychians suggested. The person of Christ is 'one person in two natures' and these two natures are combined in a way which doesn't result in their being confused with each other or changed into each other, but in a way which makes them indivisible and inseparable from each other. Christ's divine and human natures are united 'unconfusedly, unchangeably, indivisibly, inseparably'. This was the

Church's conclusion after generations of debate, at the Council of Chalcedon in 451: one person in two natures. Thus what can be said of Christ's human nature can be said of his whole person, because he is only one person. For instance, it can properly be said that God the Son truly grieves, suffers and dies in the one person of Jesus Christ.

Who is it that truly undergoes the authentic and undiminished reality of human suffering? None other than the divine Son of God! What is the manner in which he undergoes the whole reality of human suffering? A human manner! Since it is actually the Son of God who lives a genuine human life, so it is the Son of God who, as man, experiences all aspects of human life, including suffering and death. In other words, *the Impassible suffers*. Saying this, as Weinandy notes, is not to be incoherent, but to state the very heart of the mystery of the incarnation.

God suffers – not in his divinity, but in his humanity. The impassible divine nature was not confused with or changed into passible human nature in the person of Christ, but the impassible divine nature was united with his human nature indivisibly and inseparably so that, as a whole person, God could suffer in Christ as a man. To replace the phrase 'the Impassible suffers' with the phrase 'the Passible suffers' is to evacuate Christ's suffering of its significance. Remember that line from the great Wesley hymn: ''Tis mystery all, the Immortal dies!' There would be nothing remarkable about saying the mortal dies; likewise there would be nothing remarkable about saying the passible suffers. By dissolving the mystery, Theopaschitism makes easy and plausible what in reality is the deepest, most staggering and humbling Christian mystery of all: God, the impassible, suffers as a man.

And in any case, what help would God be to us if he suffered as God? If the Son of God were to suffer in his divine nature *simpliciter*, that suffering would no longer be an authentic divine sharing in human suffering, but would be an ontologically unique and remote kind of suffering, entirely separate from human experience. And if this were so, we could not say, as Moltmann rightly wants to be able to say, by analogy with the crucifixion, that 'That youth, hanging on the gallows, is God', but instead would be required to say, 'That youth is *not* actually that youth, but God'; and that would be Docetic, a mere appearance of humanity, not the reality. True love is shown not because God as some wholly different ontological entity suffers at least *as much as* we do. True love is shown in that God suffers *in the same way* we do – in our humanity, which he shares in the person of God the incarnate Son. This he does, in the words of the Athanasian Creed (a statement of faith drawn up in about the year 500), 'not by conversion of the Godhead into flesh' – not by confusing his nature with ours or changing his nature into ours – 'but by taking of the Manhood into God' – by uniting our nature indivisibly and inseparably with his in the one person of Jesus Christ.

A popular hymn about the cross, Stuart Townend's 'How deep the Father's love for us', contains the line: 'It was my sin that held him there'. Oh, that our sin had such power! But does it? Can God be controlled like that? The passage from John's Gospel quoted at the head of this chapter reminds us that the divine nature is essentially free from human manipulation, even as it is scourged and struck. Jesus told Pilate: 'You would have no power over me unless it had been given you from above.' It wasn't our sin that propelled Christ to the cross, but divine love, his unchangeable and unchanging love. Out of his own freedom the impassible and loving God *chose* to suffer in our humanity and to take upon himself our sin. This mysterious, holy and life-giving choice of his is the one 'heresy' we have not to avoid, but to embrace.

Part 2

HERESIES OF THE CHURCH AND CHRISTIAN LIVING

AND HOW TO AVOID THEM

———————

7

Marcionism:
Can Christians dispense with
the God of the Old Testament?

ANGELA TILBY

What is Marcionism?

Marcionism is the heresy which asserts that the God of the Old Testament has nothing to do with the Gospel of Jesus Christ. It is named after Marcion, a native of Sinope on the Black Sea, a wealthy shipowner and son of a bishop, who died in about 160. Marcion attached himself to the church in Rome and then organized his followers as a separate community, achieving a widespread influence. He was opposed by many leaders of the early Church, including Irenaeus of Lyons, Tertullian at Carthage, and Clement and Origen at Alexandria. He was formally excommunicated in 144.

*　*　*

Key Scriptures

Now when all the people perceived the thunderings and the lightnings and the sound of the trumpet and the mountain smoking, the people were afraid and trembled; and they stood afar off, and said to Moses, 'You speak to us, lest we die.' And Moses said to the people, 'Do not fear; for God has come to prove you, and that the fear of him may be before your eyes, that you may not sin.' (Exodus 20.18–21)

'Think not that I have come to abolish the law and the prophets; I have come not to abolish them but to fulfil them. For truly, I say to you, till heaven and earth pass away, not an iota, not a dot, will pass from the law until all is accomplished. Whoever then relaxes one of the least of these commandments and teaches men so, shall be called least in the kingdom of heaven; but he who does them and teaches them shall be called great in the kingdom of heaven. For I tell you, unless your righteousness exceeds that of the scribes and Pharisees, you will never enter the kingdom of heaven.' (Matthew 5.17–20)

*   *   *

The heresy of Marcion was one of the most successful of early Christian heresies, if success is judged by the strength of the opposition it provoked. Marcion's heresy was attacked by some of the most formidable Christian thinkers of the second century. Justin Martyr, Irenaeus, Tertullian, and even (the rather later) Origen all took up their theological cudgels against Marcion and his ideas. They describe him as a demonically inspired blasphemer, a mutilator of the gospel, and as a generally nasty character: vain, rich and ambitious. What had he done, you may well ask, to bring such condemnation upon himself? In our age of conspiracy theories the sheer outrage he caused might be taken as evidence that he got something important right; perhaps he had grasped some essential Christian truth which the more orthodox had overlooked or wished to repress. Well, you must judge that for yourself, and you will have plenty of opportunity to do so, because of all the early Christian heresies, Marcionism shows signs of a vigorous and continuing life.

Consider, for example, the following contemporary statements: 'The God of the Old Testament is a tyrant'; 'Jesus came to show compassion, unlike the God of wrath'; 'Love is the opposite of the law'; 'Luke's Gospel is the essence of Christianity'. All these views were originally propagated by Marcion, and together constituted a serious alternative to the development of Christian orthodoxy. Marcion came from Pontus in Asia and he established himself in Rome in about the year 140. His novel teachings led to a break with the rest of the Christian community and he was excommunicated. However, he was a good organizer and his teachings spread, enabling him to establish separate congregations in other cities of the empire.

Marcion's achievement was to find an itch within the emerging Christian orthodoxy which he felt compelled to scratch. He revealed the nature of this itch in a book which he called *Antitheses*, which is best translated as 'contradictions'. For him there was a fundamental contradiction between law and love, righteousness and grace. Marcion thought that true Christianity was flawed by the incompatibilities at the heart of its teaching. His solution was radical. Nothing less than a restatement of faith would do, and for Marcion that restatement had to focus on what for him was the essential gospel: the love, mercy and compassion displayed in the life and teachings of Jesus. This, for him, was all that was necessary, it was the blueprint for a new and pure humanity. There was no other truly Christian foundation for belief or morality.

What Marcion couldn't bear was the note of judgement that went along with the preaching of the Christian message, the warnings that came with the teaching of the law, the call to obedience and the threat of hell. For Marcion, the picture of God given in the passage from the book of Exodus quoted at the head of this chapter, a God whose presence is manifest in thunder and lightning and smoke on the mountain, was simply unbelievable. A God who makes his people tremble with fear, a God with whom they are afraid to communicate, could not be the God and Father of the Lord Jesus Christ. In fact, passages like this seemed to him to cast doubt on the central claim of the gospel. As he saw it, the Christianity of his day needed purging so that the pure gospel could be received in all its radical simplicity and appeal to the heart.

Marcion was convinced that the cause of the contradictions in the Church's message lay in the Old Testament and that Christianity could be freed from its errors only if it detached itself from its Jewish heritage. So he set out to prove that the Old Testament was indeed contradicted by the New, and that the character of God in the Old Testament was incompatible with the character of God proclaimed by Jesus. The God of the Old Testament, he claimed, was unworthy of Christian worship. First, God was ignorant: Marcion pointed out that in the book of Genesis (1.9) God had to ask Adam where he was, proving that his knowledge was limited. Second, he was immoral; for had not God rewarded David, who was adulterous and acquis-itive (2 Samuel 5—24)? Third, God was inconsistent: having forbidden the use of images he instructed the Israelites to erect a brass serpent on a pole (Numbers 21.8). Marcion's conclu-sion was that the creator God of the Old Testament was an inferior deity who had nothing to do with the kindly Father of our Lord Jesus Christ. In his view, the whole purpose of the mission of Jesus was to rescue us from the domination of the Old Testament God. So the answer for Marcion was to discard the Old Testament. But then he had to go further because, as is obvious from the Matthew passage quoted at the head of this chapter, Jesus preached continuity with the revelation given to the Jews: he came not to abolish the law and the prophets, but to fulfil them. For Marcion, this was simply unacceptable. The Saviour simply could not have preached such a thing. The only explanation was that the Jews had somehow got hold of the Gospel texts and corrupted them. So thorough was the corrup-tion of the Gospels that Marcion decided that only the Gospel of Luke did real justice to the Christian revelation, and even that needed editing! He accepted the letters of Paul, but, once again, edited out anything which suggested that the law might have been given by God and still had a part to play in the life of the redeemed. Thus Marcion drew up his simple, common-sense, down-to-earth version of Christian piety, shorn of its contradictions, a testament, as he saw it, to the pure love and compassion of God in Jesus Christ.

Now there are aspects of this teaching which come extraordinarily close to what a lot of Christians, both of our own time and of earlier ages, have believed and do believe. The itch that Marcion scratched has never quite gone away. Many Christians have problems with the God of thunder and darkness who gave the law on Sinai, the God who revels in the glories of his own creation, the God who smites his enemies on the jawbone and takes vengeance upon the third and fourth generations of those who displease him. When Julian of Norwich insisted that there is no wrath in God she was giving voice to the discomfort many have always felt when confronted with the character of God in the Old Testament. Marcion's denigration of the law anticipates the revolt of Martin Luther, who hated the law almost as much as Marcion did, and took refuge, like Marcion, in the letters of Paul, particularly the letter to the Romans. But Luther was not a true Marcionite. It was Rome he hated, not the text of Scripture, and he did not deny the goodness of creation.

Marcion's beliefs are rather closer to the later liberal Protestantism that flourished at the end of the nineteenth century in Germany. It is hardly surprising that it was the great German theologian, Adolf von Harnack, who attempted to rehabilitate Marcion in a book published in 1921. Von Harnack's version of Christianity was ethical and undogmatic, a proclamation of the universal Fatherhood of God and the brotherhood of man. Indeed, I can feel the temptation to Marcionism myself when confronted with the sheer nastiness of some contemporary strands of Christianity: the bullying that masks itself as righteous orthodoxy, the persecution of those striving for honesty in areas that embarrass or expose the Church. What the ultra-conservative (or the merely timid and compliant) fail to realize is that a Christianity which wields its moral and dogmatic authority like a hammer actually sows despair in the hearts of the faithful to the point where faith is destroyed. One thinks of figures like Bishop Richard Holloway, now virtually an atheist, or David Jenkins, the former bishop of Durham, whose liberal views became more extreme as he clashed with supposedly orthodox Christianity. Marcion's protest exposes a genuinely raw nerve.

At the same time I am glad that his views did not prevail. It is sometimes claimed that liberals have an unnerving capacity for intolerance, and, in his way Marcion was something of an intellectual bully; his radicalism, if accepted, would have destroyed the faith of the less than confident. Marcion's purified Christianity, for all its emphasis on love, was not without an element of hatred, particularly towards the Jews. Marcion abhorred the favoured status of the Jewish people; it was for him an example of the Creator's sheer bad taste and lack of intelligence to select one human group for special attention. Marcion suspected that it was Jews who had corrupted the New Testament, and so he dismissed any scriptural evidence, even in the writings of his favourites Paul and Luke, which suggested that the coming of Christ was a prophetic fulfilment of the old covenant. He had no room in his mind for the biblical text to have layers of meaning, for symbol or allegory. He had no sympathy for arguments like those of Origen who suggested that the exaggerations and contradictions in Scripture are intended to point to truths which are beyond our capacity to grasp by common sense. Marcion, in other words, was a literalist, who rejected what he could not accept in the Bible with the same kind of fervour and lack of nuance as a conservative fundamentalist might display in accepting everything. *horrindo*

What Marcion really rejected was creation. He was appalled by sex and denigrated marriage. He could not bear the thought that Jesus had been born of a woman. To him, the messiness of sex and birth could only belong to the botched world of the Old Testament creator. His disgust for the material world lay behind his rejection of the law. His antinomianism (the belief that because of grace Christians do not have to observe moral law) is not so much a charter for freedom as a rejection of a world in which moral choice and growth in virtue is required of human beings. Marcion thought the only goodness worth having was that grounded in a spontaneous response to the love of Christ. He had no real interest in law as a divine gift given to enable people to live decently, and within proper boundaries, not as angels but as human beings. You get the impression that Marcion wanted to be an angel, a pure spirit, not limited by the body and its needs. So it is not surprising to find that his image of the Saviour also falls short of orthodoxy; Marcion's Christ is a kind of angelic figure, not a true human being at all. His views represent the outworking in Christian living of the Docetic heresy.

I said that Marcion anticipates some aspects of liberal Protestantism and perhaps that thought needs to be justified. His rejection of the revealed law, the Old Testament, and created nature anticipates not only some aspects of Luther and von Harnack's thought but a cluster of contemporary theological trends as well. In my experience there are certain kinds of apparently liberal theology which take themselves very seriously indeed and *know* which parts of the Bible are authentic and which have been corrupted. They *know* what Jesus really taught and what the early Church added on. In the 1990s there was a group of New Testament scholars in the United States who gave themselves the name of 'The Jesus Seminar'. They produced a version of the Gospels with the few sayings they believed to be original to Jesus marked in red. The Jesus of 'The Jesus Seminar' was a wise peasant with a humane and universal message, who also happened to be antinomian and anti-authoritarian and whose Jewishness, while not denied, was significantly played down.

Those who produce versions of Christianity like this tend to be very earnest. There is no room for playfulness or humour; they know they are right, because contradiction and inconsistency have been ironed out. Latter-day Marcionites are over-idealistic about human beings; they preach spontaneity and love, and they reject dogma and rules. The notion of sin is regarded with a certain scorn as a primitive idea which no longer resonates. Yet, inside the apparent generosity of Marcionism there is a terrible demand made on human beings to deny the contradictions within human nature, to smooth over the troubling parts of the human equation in such a way that aggression and ambition, competitiveness and sexual desire are all faintly suspect. As well as having no sense of humour this kind of Christianity tends to persecute those who cannot share its vision of a pure, idealized humanity.

So how can we avoid Marcionism? A useful diagnostic test for Marcionite Christianity is the presence of anti-Semitism. Luther was vehemently anti-Semitic; Adolf von Harnack also had anti-Semitic tendencies, which can be seen in the sheer fact that Nazi ideology was able to develop quite comfortably within the setting of German liberal Protestantism. When the apparent liberalism of the Church begins to express itself in a suspicion of Jewish life and Jewish thought, the ghost of Marcionism is waiting in the wings. The antidote is to embrace the fundamentals: the goodness of creation, the blessing of the law, the history of redemption, seeing not the contradictions but the continuities. As Irenaeus insisted in his *Against Heresies*, redemption does not involve an escape from material life, but an immersion in God's saving purpose for the world which culminates in the incarnation. We are not to seek angelic purity of race or of 'spirit', but the glory of God which is, as Irenaeus also reminds us, 'the human person fully alive'. So beware of any form of Christianity which interprets what it is to be a human being in generalized, idealized terms; that makes no room for the particular, the idiosyncratic, the strange, the peculiar. For Marcionism is, above all, tidy, and whenever it recurs it wants to sweep away anything which does not conform. Beware of Christianity when it claims to have all the answers to the human condition. It usually means it has not understood the question posed to us by our creation, by the mystery of Scripture and the astonishing gospel of Christ in which the divine is not compromised by what is human and the human is not annihilated by what is divine.

8

Donatism:
Do Christian ministers need to be faultless for their ministrations to be effective?

BEN QUASH

———✦———

What is Donatism?

Donatism is the schismatic heresy which holds that the Church must remain 'holy' according to Donatist rather than catholic standards, and that sacraments conferred by those deemed to be 'unholy' are invalid. It arose in North Africa in the early fourth century and is named after Donatus, a bishop whom the Donatists supported in opposition to Caecilian, whose consecration they objected to because his consecrator, Felix of Aptunga, had been a *traditor* (one who handed over church property) during the persecution of Christians conducted under the Roman Emperor Diocletian (284–305). They were opposed chiefly by Augustine of Hippo, who maintained that the unworthiness of the minister does not affect the validity of the sacraments since their true minister is Christ. The Donatists were condemned by the Synod of Arles in 314.

* * *

Key Scriptures

And the LORD said to Moses, 'Say to all the congregation of the people of Israel, You shall be holy; for I the LORD your God am holy.

'. . . You shall not steal, nor deal falsely, nor lie to one another. And you shall not swear by my name falsely, and so profane the name of your God: I am the LORD.

'. . . You shall not hate your brother in your heart, but you shall reason with your neighbour, lest you bear sin because of him. You shall not take vengeance or bear any grudge against the sons of your own people, but you shall love your neighbour as yourself: I am the LORD.

'You shall keep my statutes. You shall not let your cattle breed with a different kind; you shall not sow your field with two kinds of seed; nor shall there come upon you a garment of cloth made of two kinds of stuff.

'. . . When a stranger sojourns with you in your land, you shall not do him wrong. The stranger who sojourns with you shall be to you as the native among you, and you shall love him as yourself; for you were strangers in the land of Egypt: I am the LORD your God.

'You shall do no wrong in judgment, in measures of length or weight or quantity. You shall have just balances, just weights, a just ephah, and a just hin: I am the LORD your God, who brought you out of the land of Egypt. And you shall observe all my statutes and all my ordinances, and do them: I am the LORD.' (Leviticus 19.1–2, 11–12, 17–19, 33–37)

Another parable he put before them, saying, 'The kingdom of heaven may be compared to a man who sowed good seed in his field; but while men were sleeping, his enemy came and sowed weeds among the wheat, and went away. So when the plants came up and bore grain, then the weeds appeared also. And the servants of the householder came and said to him, "Sir, did you not sow good seed in your field? How then has it weeds?" He said to them, "An enemy has done this." The servants said to him, "Then do you want us to go and gather them?" But he said, "No; lest in gathering the weeds you root up the wheat along with them. Let both grow together until the harvest; and at harvest time I will tell the reapers, Gather the weeds first and bind them in bundles to be burned, but gather the wheat into my barn."' (Matthew 13.24–30)

* * *

Some heresies are major movements in the history of Western thought and some of them are more obscure thought-experiments by small groups of the religiously peculiar. In this chapter I am going to tackle a big one, whose consequences are still very present to the Church, and important for it. It is Donatism – technically, perhaps, a schism rather than a heresy, for the rent it caused in the one, holy, catholic and apostolic Church was not first and foremost doctrinal. Ecclesiological convention has it that whereas heresy is opposed to faith, schism is opposed to love, and Irenaeus in his master-work, *Against Heresies*, lends his authority to this distinction when he refers to the loveless-ness of schismatics:

> [God] shall also judge those who give rise to schisms, who are destitute of the love of God, and who look to their own special advantage rather than to the unity of the Church; and who for trifling reasons, or any kind of reason which occurs to them, cut in pieces and divide the great and glorious body of Christ. (*Against Heresies*, Book IV, Chapter 3, paragraph 7)

Of course the schismatics we call Donatists would not for a moment have accepted that they were acting for 'trifling reasons'; as we shall see, they had what was in many ways an admirably serious attitude to church discipline. Yet it was a question of church discipline, exacerbated by political and, perhaps, economic tensions, that ignited the powder keg we now call the Donatist controversy, and this is what those who like to police the technical border between heresy and schism will point to when they deny Donatism the status of heresy proper.

Nonetheless, the border between schism and heresy is a blurry one. And in fact, one of the instructive features of the Donatist dispute as a whole is precisely the way it highlights the artificiality of separating faith (or belief) from love (or prac-tice). Christian practice is itself a sort of theology, an exposi-tion. To those who saw themselves as the loyal 'catholics' in this controversy, Donatism offended against *both* proper Church order *and* true Church teaching, and the Donatists thought the same in reverse. And even if it didn't begin as a dispute about theology narrowly conceived (that is, conceived as something to do with a realm of intellectual ideas as distinct from practices), substantial theological guns would eventually be wheeled out on both sides of this dispute, so that in many ways Donatism's opponents gave it the same treatment as any heretical departure from the Church's true teaching.

What was Donatism all about? To answer this I need to transport you to North Africa in the very early years of the fourth century, some thirty years before the birth of Augustine of Hippo – who was later to play such a key role in the controversy. The Christians in North Africa at the time, as elsewhere in the Roman Empire, were living in the aftermath of terrible persecution – the Great Persecution carried out under the pagan emperor Diocletian, who declared himself a demigod and didn't like rivals. Church buildings were demolished, and their sacred books and vessels confiscated or burned. Clergy who resisted were imprisoned, tortured and in many cases killed. The martyrs were revered as heroes by many Christians in North Africa, and those who survived imprisonment and torture were honoured with the title 'Confessor'. But some clergy had capitulated, complying with instructions from the persecutors and handing over church property. They were called *traditores*, or 'hander-overs'.

In his book *Augustine* (Oxford, 1986), Henry Chadwick describes how in the fourth century, as now, there were hawks and doves in most spheres of public life and the Church was no exception. The Christian hawks had never been keen on cooperating with secular authority; they expected the end of the world soon in any case, and saw themselves as 'safeguarding the authentic holiness and ritual purity of God's Temple, the Church' until his coming – at whatever cost, and without fear of confrontation and reprisals. They wanted nothing more to do with the hander-overs, the *traditores*. The doves, meanwhile, 'wanted no confrontations, but only to live quiet lives of modest virtue' and ordered faithfulness. They were prepared to let the *traditores* return to ministry and carry on.

In 311 a big church vacancy came up in North Africa: the bishop of Carthage died, and his post needed to be filled. The doves moved fast and gathered three bishops to consecrate the archdeacon as his successor. But it was widely believed that the principal consecrator was one of the bishops who eight years before had surrendered church property to the confiscating authorities, i.e. he was a *traditor*. As a consequence, the hawks would not recognize the consecration as valid, and immediately consecrated a rival bishop. After some 'uneasy negotiations', as Chadwick recounts, this rival bishop (the hawks' bishop, whose name was Majorinus) was refused recognition by the churches north of the Mediterranean, including Rome, and by the new Emperor, Constantine the Great. He was not acknowledged as the 'catholic' bishop – the one in communion with the Church Universal. This strengthened further the hawks' sense that they represented an authentic and indigenous African Christianity that was being unjustly put upon by alien forces that had no rightful claim on them – one of those forces being state power with which for good reasons of raw recent memory they wanted no truck. As Chadwick puts it: 'From thenceforth until the Muslim invasion of Africa [three and a half centuries later] two rival groups existed, each with its own episcopate, each reciting the same creed, each with identical sacramental forms and liturgical structures. Altar was erected against altar in every city and village.' The successor to that first hawks' bishop in Carthage was called Donatus, and that's why Donatism has the name it does.

A number of the authors in this book note that heretics often had good points to make, and it's easy to understand what made the Donatists so passionate about their position. They had held fast to the faith in the face of terrible persecution. They had risked their lives. They took with absolute seriousness the divine call we hear, for example, in the book of Leviticus: 'Be holy, for I am holy' (Leviticus 11.44). They were rigorists. They believed in the perfection of the Church, and quoted the saying that the Church is 'without spot or blemish' (2 Peter 3.14). Perhaps theirs was an anger not wholly unlike the anger Christians in parts of Africa feel today towards their fellow religionists in the West. They face daily violence, and the loss of their churches, schools and hospitals at the hands of militant Islam. Then they look at what they see as the Western churches' compromise with worldliness, and accommodation to secular or irreligious ideas and ways of life, and they feel anger – and their instinct is to break communion. In that sense, the problems faced by the Anglican Communion today are not new problems.

The bitterness of the split North Africa saw in the fourth century had terrible consequences, however, from which nobody benefited. In the years that followed the initial schism, the rigorism of the Donatists found expression in actions that were far from holy. Gangs of marauding Donatist thugs called *circumcelliones* would smash catholic basilicas, and maim, kill and ambush catholic clergy – sometimes throwing a mixture of lime and vinegar in their eyes to blind them. Augustine himself once escaped a Donatist ambush intended to silence him for ever, but only because his guide mistook the road. And the core theological issue at the heart of it all – the nub of the matter – was this: they refused to acknowledge the validity of catholic sacraments of any kind, not baptism, not the Eucharist, not ordination – *nothing* – because of what certain of its bishops were meant to have done under the persecutions in previous years. They thought the catholic Church had become polluted by the actions of those bishops. They thought that bishops and priests who had erred, or acted sinfully – the hander-overs above all – could not from that point onwards have functioned in any meaningful way in the true Church. From that point onwards, however faithful and good a person going forward for ordination might be, he was not really ordained if ordained by a bad bishop, or even if ordained by somebody in communion with a bad bishop. Likewise, even a devout communicant living a holy life was not really receiving communion if receiving it from a bad priest, or from a priest ordained by a bad bishop. And those baptized in the polluted catholic Church needed rebaptism, according to the Donatists. Only the Donatists were pure; only they were the true Church (they would not have conceded that the catholics had better rights than they did to the title 'catholic'.)

And when asked whether God could really have intended his Universal Church to be reduced to one limited area of Africa, the Donatists argued, in Chadwick's words, that 'on moral issues, minorities are generally right, the silent majority being another name for spineless compromisers'. They pointed to Noah's Ark as a prefiguration of redemption through the one Church of Christ, and took satisfaction from pointing out that the Ark only contained eight people.

The crucial arguments advanced in return – and most decisively of all by Augustine – drew inspiration from the other text that appears at the head of this chapter: the parable of the Wheat and the Tares. The Donatists had what we might call a Levitical passion for purity and separation ('You shall not let your cattle breed with a different kind; you shall not sow your field with two kinds of seed', Leviticus 19.19) – a passion, we may note in passing, that seems unnaturally detached from attention to the duty to love their neighbour and care for the stranger in their land, on which Leviticus is equally clear. But in Matthew's parable the servants of the householder who want to go out immediately and pull up all the weeds from among the wheat are *rebuked*. 'Let both grow together', says the householder, 'until the harvest; and at harvest time I will tell the reapers, Gather the weeds first and bind them in bundles to be burned, but gather the wheat into my barn' (Matthew 13.30). The Donatists interpreted the field in the parable as representing the *world*, not the Church. Good and bad may well coexist in the *world*, they thought – for the Church must live alongside pagans – but the tares stand for those *outside* the Church. Those inside the Church must be pure wheat. Augustine, meanwhile, interprets the field as the *Church itself*. The tares are inside the Church as well as outside it, and we have to live with that until the end of time.

Perhaps embarrassingly for those of us who stand in the tradition Augustine helped to define as catholic on this issue, the Donatist interpretation represents the rather more accurate use of Scripture than the catholic one, for Jesus himself says in interpreting the parable that the field is indeed the 'world'. And there are other embarrassments in the full story of how catholics dealt with Donatists – not least the sporadic but devastating deployment of imperial force to suppress them, with full ecclesial sanction (that too hardly embodying the Levitical call to love one's neighbour as oneself, and being perhaps one of the least defensible positions Augustine ever allowed himself to advocate). And in lots of ways the Donatists (at least those not marauding or supporting the marauders) embodied just that proper emphasis on right practice as inseparable from Christian truth which we acknowledged at the beginning of this chapter. They wanted, at their best, to be disciplined communities of character.

The problem was that their practice betrayed two things at the heart of Christian teaching: the ineradicable fallibility of creation (*including* the Church) and its consequent unavoidable need of grace on this side of the end of time. It is God's job to make the Church pure, not ours, and he will do it when he is ready. However morally zealous we are, we will never by our own effort carve out a pure space which we can call the *true* Church by pointing to the unimpeachable lives of its members. Instead, they will sin, and they will need to be forgiven, and they will do so constantly. The holiness of the Church is precisely that it is a place where this circulation of forgiveness goes on all the time; it is not because forgiveness is never necessary in the first place. A Church which insisted that its members –

or even just its clergy – had to be spotless would be an empty Church, or else a dishonest Church. We may not like *traditores*, and there may even be sins for which we need to excommunicate them and people like them, but we cannot say that the baptisms they have administered and the Eucharists they have presided over and the ordinations they have performed are null and void, and that all who have dealings with them automatically place *themselves* outside the Church too. And, paradoxically, even being schismatic has never for the Church catholic entailed of necessity the loss of orders.

The great result for the Christian Church of defeating Donatism was that it could establish the following principle – in practice and in teaching – which you'll find repeated and upheld in the Book of Common Prayer of the Church of England too, as well as in most other Christian denominations: the grace of God in the sacraments does not depend for its efficacy on the personal sanctity of the individual minister, but on whether in the sacramental actions (Baptism or Eucharist, for example) he does what God commands to be done. It is not just the minister who acts in the sacramental action, but the whole Church. And ultimately, 'the sacrament is Christ's, not the minister's personal property, and salvation is always and throughout the work of God, not of man'; thus Chadwick. Or, in the words of the 39 Articles in the Book of Common Prayer, 'the Unworthiness of the Ministers . . . hinders not the effect of the Sacrament':

> Although in the visible Church the evil be ever mingled with the good, and sometimes the evil have chief authority in the Ministration of the Word and Sacraments, yet forasmuch as they do not the same in their own name, but in Christ's, and do minister by his commission and authority, we may use their Ministry, both in hearing the Word of God, and in receiving of the Sacraments. Neither is the effect of Christ's ordinance taken away by their wickedness, nor the grace of God's gifts diminished from such as by faith and rightly do receive the

Sacraments ministered unto them; which be effectual, because of Christ's institution and promise, although they be ministered by evil men. (Book of Common Prayer, Article 26)

This is a great comfort to those who are ordained!

In a sense, what was at stake in the battle between the Donatists and the catholic Church of Augustine's day was how the *ultimate* (God's perfected Kingdom at the end of time, which the Church points to) relates to the *penultimate* (our life in time and in human flesh, looking towards what is to come but not pretending it is already here). Dietrich Bonhoeffer explored this in a famous passage on the tension between radicalism and compromise. In his book, *Ethics*, he wrote:

Radicalism sees God as Judge and Redeemer; compromise sees God as Creator and Preserver. In Radicalism the end is rendered absolute; in compromise, things as-they-are are rendered absolute. Radicalism hates time; compromise hates eternity. Radicalism hates patience; compromise hates decision. Radicalism hates wisdom; compromise hates simplicity. Radicalism hates moderation and measure; compromise hates the immeasurable. Radicalism hates the real; compromise hates the Word. (Dietrich Bonhoeffer, *Ethics* (London, 1955, p. 130))

The ultimate can be made the enemy of the penultimate – that's radicalism in Bonhoeffer's sense, and that, I think, was the Donatists' mistake. The penultimate can be made the enemy of the ultimate – that's compromise and that is a risk the Church constantly faces, tempted as she is to baptize the *status quo* and go for the most comfortable option, forgetting that there is a great judgement coming and that God intends to make all things new. But God's will is that the ultimate and the penultimate be allowed to serve each other: the penultimate taking on significance and definition from what it is moving towards; the ultimate giving space and time to the created order for its response, being merciful to its mistakes, loving it. For the ultimate is no less ultimate because it is patient with what is other than itself – and that is one of the greatest Christian teachings of all.

9

Pelagianism:
Can people be saved by
their own efforts?

NICHOLAS ADAMS

———◆·◆·◆———

What is Pelagianism?

Pelagianism is the heresy which implicitly denies the existence
of original sin and asserts that people can take the initial steps
towards salvation by their own efforts, choosing the good by
virtue of their created natures. It is named after Pelagius, a
British theologian who taught in Rome in the late fourth and
early fifth centuries. Pelagianism was opposed chiefly by Augustine of Hippo and was officially condemned by Zosimus, the
bishop of Rome, in 418.

*   *   *

Key Scriptures

Naaman, commander of the army of the king of Syria, was a great
man with his master and in high favour, because by him the LORD
had given victory to Syria. He was a mighty man of valour, but
he was a leper. Now the Syrians on one of their raids had carried
off a little maid from the land of Israel, and she waited on
Naaman's wife. She said to her mistress, 'Would that my lord were
with the prophet who is in Samaria! He would cure him of his
leprosy.' So Naaman went in and told his lord, 'Thus and so spoke
the maiden from the land of Israel.' And the king of Syria said,
'Go now, and I will send a letter to the king of Israel.'

. . . So Naaman came with his horses and chariots and halted at the door of Elisha's house. And Elisha sent a messenger to him, saying, 'Go and wash in the Jordan seven times, and your flesh shall be restored, and you shall be clean.' But Naaman was angry, and went away, saying, 'Behold, I thought that he would surely come out to me, and stand, and call on the name of the LORD his God, and wave his hand over the place, and cure the leper. Are not Abana and Pharpar, the rivers of Damascus, better than all the waters of Israel? Could I not wash in them, and be clean?' So he turned and went away in a rage. But his servants came near and said to him, 'My father, if the prophet had commanded you to do some great thing, would you not have done it? How much, rather, then, when he says to you, "Wash, and be clean"?' So he went down and dipped himself seven times in the Jordan, according to the word of the man of God; and his flesh was restored like the flesh of a little child, and he was clean. (2 Kings 5.1–5, 9–14)

What then? Are we Jews any better off? No, not at all; for I have already charged that all men, both Jews and Greeks, are under the power of sin, as it is written:

> 'None is righteous, no, not one;
> no one understands, no one seeks for God.
> All have turned aside, together they have gone wrong;
> no one does good, not even one.'

. . . Now we know that whatever the law says it speaks to those who are under the law, so that every mouth may be stopped, and the whole world may be held accountable to God. For no human being will be justified in his sight by works of the law, since through the law comes knowledge of sin.

But now the righteousness of God has been manifested apart from law, although the law and the prophets bear witness to it, the righteousness of God through faith in Jesus Christ for all who believe. For there is no distinction; since all have sinned and fall short of the glory of God, they are justified by his grace as a gift, through the redemption which is in Christ Jesus, whom God put forward as an expiation by his blood, to be received by faith. This was to show God's righteousness, because in his divine forbearance he had passed over former sins; it was to prove at the present time that he himself is righteous and that he justifies him who has faith in Jesus.

Then what becomes of our boasting? It is excluded. On what principle? On the principle of works? No, but on the principle of faith. For we hold that a man is justified by faith apart from works of law. (Romans 3.9–12, 19–28)

* * *

Before looking at what Pelagians actually believed, it will be useful to consider the way in which they put forward their case and the way in which their views were opposed. The orthodox opponents of Pelagius and his followers found that their heretical beliefs could not be dismissed easily because they used careful, well thought-out arguments. And this forces us to ask what our Christian calling is in response to beliefs that are – so it seems to us, the orthodox – wrong.

One answer is to annihilate these views using all available measures. We should make them seem stupid and ill-considered. To do this, we would have to misrepresent them. If we have a book written by a heretic, we could go to trial and quote misleadingly from it, take things out of context, exaggerate claims that in fact were rather muted, and mute the claims that were at its core. We could discredit the character of the writer, and show how his disreputable life calls his writing and thinking into question. We could try not only to condemn their writings, but have them expelled bodily from the Church. Then, after the trial, we could write it up, in our own words, and cause the original texts to vanish. We could justify our actions on the grounds that we were protecting future generations from error. This is what, more or less, happened to Arius (see Chapter 1).

A quite different strategy would be to tackle the thinking head-on and show that our – orthodox – views are more sensible and that our arguments are better thought out. This would be to take our opponents seriously. Instead of besmirching the character of our opponents, we could draw attention to their fine qualities. Instead of misreading and misquoting, we could pay extra special attention to their texts. Instead of destroying those texts, we could try to reproduce their thinking faithfully in our own. And instead of trying to expel them from the Church we could try to find ways to include them in the community of faith.

Now all this probably seems wildly idealistic. Yet this is, by and large, how Augustine approached the heresy of Pelagianism. He reproduced its arguments rather well; he referred to his opponents as having 'the strongest and quickest wits [*fortissima et celerrima ingenia*]'; and he tried not to expel them from the Church but to change their minds through argumentation.

Notice that the virtue Augustine attributes to Pelagians is intelligence. We may nervously wonder whether Augustine is suggesting that intelligence is not such a virtue after all, but is rather part of the problem. Is he suggesting that intelligence causes, or at least exacerbates, heresy – that heretics are too clever for their own good? We feel uncomfortable because we – the orthodox – aspire to intelligence. What if being orthodox means being willing not to think too hard? Well, we should be reassured, because that is far from Augustine's line of attack. He is certainly frustrated that the intelligence of the Pelagians should be directed to such problematic ends, but he does not enjoin his readers to dumb down in the interests of right thinking. Augustine tries to raise the level of debate. And instead of closing things down, he tries to understand the disagreements and expound his opponents' views, in order to show the problem. Augustine's approach to heresy – or at least to this heresy – was to prolong debate rather than to cut it off. Intelligence, then, is not just a Pelagian attribute; it is an orthodox virtue.

To understand the relationship between the Church and heretics we can draw upon a modern-day phenomenon familiar to us all, the daytime TV show. Let's consider 'Dr Phil' McGraw, a 'Texan' psychiatrist (who was actually born in Oklahoma), who has a series spun off from *The Oprah Winfrey Show*. Dr Phil invites guests with problems on to his show so that he can help them. When I was watching, Graham and Sophie (names changed) were his guests. Sophie was complaining that Graham refused to take her out to dinner any more. They were now in their late twenties, and were thus 'old'. When they had been 'young' and were dating, Graham used to take her out all the time. Now, whenever Sophie suggests it, he says, 'you choose where we go'. Sophie was very frustrated, because the 'magic' had gone out: she wanted Graham to surprise her, to decide for himself where to go, and to whisk her off. She mounted a fierce critique of her husband, exposing his shortcomings, lamenting the wasteland of their marriage, and pronounced a damning sentence on Graham's inability to take the initiative. Dr Phil suggested, mildly, that perhaps she could do more to encourage her husband. Sophie launched another fierce and minutely observed critique. Dr Phil switched posture dramatically and in loud confrontational mode, asked: 'Do you want to be right, or do you want to eat dinner in a nice restaurant with your husband?'

I'm not sure that Pelagianism makes good daytime TV (if anything does). But Sophie's marriage to Graham is something like the relationship between the Pelagians and the Church: they want to be together, but they face challenges in getting along. Sophie is in danger of being a heretic: she wants to be right so much that she is willing to risk the health of her relationship. This is not an entirely bad model of what catholicity is about. We meet together to break bread. This is what we want to do: it's what we really want. It is good to share in the Eucharist, and participate in God's healing action in the world. There is nothing more important to us than this. And yet, at the same time, we want to be right. The problem with heretics is that they often want to be right even if it means they can't break bread with their fellow Christians. The problem with Church authorities, from time to time, is that they are willing to excommunicate potential heretics without properly evaluating their arguments. This leads to a cycle of heavy-handedness and petulant rebellion that is familiar in households with teenagers and in synods alike.

Pelagianism means *wanting to be right* about the relationship between sin and grace. One might think this is hardly a bad thing: surely all theologians should want this. The point is that Pelagians tend to want to be right rather than to do justice to the complexities of sin and grace. The standard account of Pelagian claims is, broadly, that human beings do not need grace to overcome sin, and that there is no original sin that affects all humankind. This has some use as an *aide memoire*, but the best way to understand Pelagianism is to appreciate the obscurity of the main terms (sin and grace) in the fifth century, and to see the heresy as a bid for clarity. The commonly held view at the time – between the years 400 and 411 – was that all humans were born into sin, because of Adam's sin as narrated in Genesis, and that all humans needed God's grace in order to be saved from their sin. Then, as now, things are somewhat hazy when you try to pin down certain questions. What is 'sin'? Is it 'transmitted' from Adam down to our own time? If so, how? What does God's grace look like? Is it inherent in creation or is it added to it? When and how and why is it added? What does it mean to be 'saved' by God? To achieve greater clarity on these things it will be necessary now (as it was then) to get into some of the details of this particular theological debate.

Augustine believed that people are not without sin, either that which they have derived from their birth, or that which they have added from their own misconduct. In other words, everyone is a sinner: they are born into sin, and they add to this with extra sins that they commit themselves. To support his argument, Augustine calls on Paul, as quoted at the head of this chapter: 'All have sinned and fall short of the glory of God, they are justified by his grace as a gift, through the redemption which is in Christ Jesus, whom God put forward as an expiation by his blood, to be received by faith' (Romans 3.23).

Paul supports his claim that 'all have sinned' by citing from the Psalms:

> The fool says in his heart, 'There is no God.'
> They are corrupt, they do abominable deeds,
> > there is none that does good.
> The Lord looks down from heaven upon the children of men,
> > to see if there are any that act wisely, that seek after God.
> They have all gone astray, they are all alike corrupt;
> > there is none that does good, no, not one. (Psalm 14.1–3)

This seems conclusive enough. However, if we use our intelligence and probe deeper we can see that Psalm 14, when read as a whole, is dealing with two quite distinct groups and not 'everyone' at all. These groups include on the one hand 'the fool', 'the corrupt' and 'the evil-doers', and on the other hand 'the Lord's people', 'the generation of the righteous', 'the poor', and 'Israel'. When Paul quotes Psalm 14, he quotes what is said about the first group: there is none [of them] that does good, no not one. About the second group we explicitly hear a promise of deliverance: 'When the Lord restores the fortunes of his people, Jacob shall rejoice, Israel shall be glad' (Psalm 14.7).

It appears that Augustine is interpreting Paul who is himself interpreting Psalm 14, and doing so in a way that is open to challenge. A counter-reading of Psalm 14 yields a different account of God's help. It is not offered to universal humankind in its state of sin, but is hoped for and anticipated by 'the generation of the righteous'. Psalm 14 has no word for sin, and no word for grace. It speaks of corruption, the terror of the corrupt when God will help the poor, and the deliverance of Israel. Corruption and deliverance. Not a vast distance from sin and grace, but admittedly rather vaguer and uncontrolled by dogmatics. Some are corrupt; some are delivered. If anything, Psalm

14 suggests that it is not the corrupt that are delivered, but the generation of the righteous. If anything, there is no hope for the sinner, if this means 'the corrupt', and only hope for 'the righteous', who are identified with the poor. In fact, Psalm 14 suggests the possibility that Israel means those who, by birth, are born righteous and are quite different from 'the fool' and 'the corrupt'.

This, then, is where our exercise of strong- and swift-wittedness leads us. It's neat and tidy. It also happens to be a Pelagian way of thinking. If one denies that original sin taints us all, or if one asserts that we can choose good or evil without God's help, then one is thinking like a Pelagian.

We should want to avoid following Pelagius because, although his arguments are pretty good, they come at a cost. Pelagianism has its eye on the details, but not on the bigger picture – it doesn't say enough. Things make sense if you only read Psalm 14, or if you only read parts of Romans 3, or if you only read parts of Augustine's writings against the Pelagians. If you only do these things, you can get a nice tidy Pelagian view with very little effort. The orthodox view about sin and grace really isn't tidy. It's messy and overwhelming. And to modern ears, its reasoning can seem weak. Paul is very selective in his use of Psalm 14; Augustine is very selective in his use of Romans 3. To understand what is controlling this selectivity is to know quite a lot about how good theology functions. Paul and Augustine don't just have their eyes on details; they have a sense of how things hang together. To Pelagian ears this sense makes no sense at all. 'We are all born into sin and can only be helped by God'? That's as bizarre as saying: however much we try to be good, we are still inextricably implicated in unjust international markets; we try to overcome this, and so we work for an international charity, but we still have to give money from charitable donations as bribes to corrupt officials, and thus contribute to that corruption; we try to overcome this, and so we work in a tiny village in a famine-ridden region, far from such officials; but we still keep for ourselves more food than we distribute to each family whose children are dying. And so it goes.

Notice that these untidy thoughts arise from saying more than one normally does. Consider this: I buy fair trade goods. But what if I say: I buy fair trade goods in supermarkets that are squeezing small farmers out of business? I have said more. Or this: I drove my seriously ill friend to hospital. I can say more: I drove my seriously ill friend to hospital in a car which belches out eight tonnes of ozone-destroying fumes each year. There is something undermining about saying more. Somehow, by considering how small things are located in larger concerns, problems emerge. Neatness smudges. Confidence wobbles.

This is how theology, particularly 'systematic' theology, works. 'Systematic' just means that minutiae are not considered neatly on their own terms. They are related to the whole picture. 'Systematic' here is close to 'holistic'. In order not to distort the whole, as soon as something particular is said, more has to be added. In the smallest things, one keeps an eye on their effect on the whole.

It is bad enough that Pelagianism, like all heresy, does not want to hear that particulars relate to the obscure whole of theology. Things get rather worse in the case of 'saying more' about our sinful lives; the 'more' gets us into trouble. If we try to tidy up our descriptions of ourselves, the problems don't just mount up: they become incapacitating. We see clearly the hopelessness of trying to lead a good life. Our entire Western civilization is possible because others do not live as we do. If we tidy up our thought about that, we are led deeper into the contradictions of our lives. Even if we were to find an idyllic city of equality, love and mutual respect, it would still be built on top of the old graveyards, filled with the bodies of those who lived before us and were hacked to pieces on the slaughter bench of history. There would be an eerie stillness in the ideal city: every last inhabitant would be fully aware of the destroyed lives of past generations that cannot be undestroyed. The weight of the evidence grinds us to a halt.

For some reason, Augustine, Paul and the Psalmist do not grind to a halt. It is not because they are tidy: they all constantly say more. It is because they have faith that there is more than they can ever say.

If it is to God, and not to our autonomous selves, that we look for healing, our speech has to be as untidy as God. Tidy minds are afflicted, as soon as they think 'more' about their lives, with a permanent melancholy that is rooted in genuine knowledge of their situation. To a tidy Pelagian, it is a kind of insanity to proclaim the joy of God's goodness at redeeming us from our inescapable sin. When the tidy modern mind contemplates earlier Christian songs it notices that some of them celebrate the day when Adam ate the apple in the Garden of Eden. The modern mind pricks up its ears. The day when Adam took the apple was blessed because it condemned humanity to sin, and this made it possible for Mary to give birth to Jesus who redeems us: rejoice! To the tidy modern mind, this is medieval madness!

But where do we – the orthodox – place ourselves, our practices, our beliefs? Perhaps we find ourselves in a more ambiguous place. Is our medieval madness shot through with a vein of modern melancholy? Or is it even the other way round: is our modern melancholy lit up occasionally by medieval madness?

We return to the question of sin and grace. Our task is to discern our calling when confronted with a Pelagianism that is neat and tidy and which – like Sophie on Dr Phil – wants to be right, at all costs. I am suggesting that we should display *fortissima et celerrima ingenia*. But this won't result in neatness: it will be about constantly saying more. And it won't be about bludgeoning each other with the weight of sin: it will be about acknowledging that, however great our sin, there is always incomparably more of God's help. That is a good start in avoiding Pelagianism. But we should not avoid Pelagians.

They are all around, especially in the Church. We should encourage them to exercise their wits too. We certainly should
not try to shut them up. The problem is not that they talk too
much: heretics don't say enough. And if they grind to a halt,
we should find no satisfaction – not even grim satisfaction –
in their despair. Like Naaman's servants, we should hold out a
hand, a hand that is not quite ours, an untidy hand, to help
them take the plunge, or even just make the next step. I think
that is our calling. Even this is too neat: are we like Naaman's
servants, or more like Naaman himself?

It is in offering and receiving help, a help that is both ours
and not ours, that we may find that we can eat together.
Sometimes, things may get so bad that we cannot eat together,
as Benedict indicates in his Rule: there comes a point when a
brother or sister must be excluded from the Eucharist. Sometimes, things may deteriorate so seriously that schism is desir-
able. But we will all need to be quite sure that we have really
understood, and faithfully reproduced, one another's arguments before we even consider this possibility. Few historical
schisms pass this test. So, by God's grace, we may be able to
eat together. The disagreements may not go away. But who
supposes that there are any communities purified of all disagreements? Our calling is to keep debates alive for as long
as we responsibly can, although no longer than that, which
is sometimes longer than we suppose, and to preserve the
minority voices even when they seem in error. If we have to
call things to a halt, we only do so for the time being. The best
settlements do justice to messy realities, rather than abolish
them with neat fantasies. Good questions, however wickedly
or foolishly posed, tend to return, often in new, perplexing
and worrying guises. But we should not be anxious. And we
should not be in too much of a rush.

We can afford to do this because there is always more to say;
and there is always more to say because there is always more
of God.

10

Gnosticism:
Can people be saved by
acquiring secret knowledge?

ANDERS BERGQUIST

What is Gnosticism?

Gnosticism is the heresy which asserts that people are saved by being initiated into a special kind of spiritual knowledge taught by a Jesus who was not fully human and did not die, and by practising special disciplines in order to effect spiritual release from the evil material realm created by the Demiurge (a Greek term meaning, literally, 'public maker') and thus bring about reunion with the transcendent Divine Being. It is named after the Greek word *gnosis*, meaning 'knowledge', and took many forms under many different teachers, chiefly Valentinus and Basilides in the early and middle parts of the second century. It was opposed by (among others) Irenaeus, Tertullian and Hippolytus, and by the end of the second century the Gnostics had mostly become a sect separate from the Church.

*   *   *

Key Scriptures

God saw everything that he had made, and behold, it was very good. (Genesis 1.31)

O Timothy, guard what has been entrusted to you. Avoid the god-less chatter and contradictions of what is falsely called knowledge [*gnosis*], for by professing it some have missed the mark as regards the faith. Grace be with you. (1 Timothy 6.20–21)

*   *   *

'Gnosticism' is a conventional and not always convenient label for a more-or-less related group of teachings which came to have a special attraction for Christians in the course of the second century. Unlike some of the other heresies discussed in this book, it is not associated with a single teacher, and its theological contours are complex and often opaque. There were many teachers who could be described as Gnostic because they offered *gnosis* (special knowledge) about the origin of the world and the destiny of the human soul, and their teachings varied. Some of them may well have actually called themselves Gnostics; if so, the label was soon generalized by their opponents to include others whose doctrines seemed to be related. 'Gnosticism' became a category created by its enemies, and the English word was not coined until the seventeenth century. But however much or little people used these labels of themselves, they are not wholly misleading: one of the important things that the Gnostic teachers had in common was their claim to have access to secret life-giving knowledge. Those who followed them would be truly 'in the know'. Gnostics did not have to develop separate assemblies for worship, or distinct ecclesiast-ical hierarchies. Ordinary gatherings of Christians could be excel-lent recruiting grounds for what was offered as the 'real' or 'full-strength' gospel. This promise of privileged knowledge, of initiation into a body of esoteric teaching, which was denied to those who were too earth-bound or unintelligent to deserve it, had its dangerous attractions. Secrets always do. So Gnostic groups could develop inside mainstream Christian commu-nities such as churches and monasteries, and not only outside them.

Much of our information about the content of the Gnostic gnosis – the actual teaching of the Gnostic masters – comes therefore from its enemies. Best-known of these opponents is Irenaeus, the Greek Christian from Asia Minor who has been referred to many times in preceding chapters, who made his way into what is now the south of France, by way of Rome, and ended as bishop of the Christian community in Lyons in the closing decades of the second century. He was dismayed by the Gnosticism he observed, both in the east and in Rome, and set himself to sift and catalogue the different Gnostic systems and to show why they were wrong – often, one suspects, imposing an order and connectedness on them which they did not have. Just a little later Clement of Alexandria, at the other end of the Mediterranean world, did not reject the category of gnosis outright, but tried to show what sort of a person a truly Christian Gnostic might be. In delineating his 'Christian Gnostic', he tells us much about what he considers the wrong sort of Gnostic, and he preserves quotations from Gnostic teachers whose writings are otherwise lost. It is mostly from Irenaeus and Clement, for example, that we get our knowledge of Valentinus, a highly respected Gnostic teacher in Rome.

But our sources of information about Gnosticism are not only derived from its opponents; we are also lucky enough to have some Gnostic texts in the original. In 1945, a collection of Gnostic books was found at Nag Hammadi in Egypt: twelve books, plus eight leaves from a thirteenth, constituting a little library of 52 Gnostic tractates. The books as they were found date from the second half of the fourth century and are written in Coptic, but many or all of them were originally composed in Greek at an earlier date. They embrace several different sorts of writing, including 'Gospels' additional to the four in the New Testament, mythological accounts of creation, and secret teachings attributed to the Apostles. The collection found at Nag Hammadi supplies in complete form both texts already known to exist (like the Gospel of Thomas) and texts previously unknown. It is of course a selection and it reflects the particular interests of whoever assembled it. The identity of the collector(s) is unknown, but we can make an educated guess. Nag Hammadi is close to a fourth-century Christian monastery at Chenoboskion. In 367, the formidable Athanasius of Alexandria circulated a letter in his diocese, listing those books which were to be regarded as belonging to the biblical canon and threatening punishments for anyone who was found to be teaching or studying different books as if they had scriptural authority. Some of the monks of Chenoboskion were perhaps studying just such books. Committed already to a highly ascetical form of Christianity, they were drawn to the exploration of these esoteric texts, with their promise of escape from the lower world of matter and the flesh. Now it was too dangerous to keep such Gnostic samizdat (underground literature) in the monastery, so someone slipped out to bury it nearby. It may seem like a scenario from *The Name of the Rose*, but it is plausible. And if the Nag Hammadi collection is only a sample, there is always the hope that similar texts will surface elsewhere, as in the much-publicized recent case of the Gospel of Judas, which is closely related to the Nag Hammadi writings in genre and content, and emerged in the clandestine Egyptian antiquities market.

What did the Gnostic teachers actually teach, so far as we can work it out from this evidence? A first impression is of a bewildering variety of mythical accounts of the creation, both of the material world and of a world of spiritual beings, and of teachings and injunctions designed to detach the Gnostic adept from commitment to the present world. There are elaborate accounts of the origin of created things, and fantastically detailed lists of heavenly beings. But behind the variety, there are some common structures of thought. The material world has a very low value. At best, it is an obstruction to the realization of our calling as human beings; at worst, it is actually evil. The material world was not made directly by God (God in the sense of the originator of all created being), but by a distinctly subordinate being in a complex hierarchy. This god is often called the *Demiurge*. It is his relative powerlessness in relation to superior beings in the hierarchy, or even his maliciousness, that accounts for evil and suffering in the world. Beyond the material world is the true, spiritual reality, which itself has a structure and a history. In the beginning was a serene primal unity, in some Gnostic systems called the *Pleroma* (the Fullness). A movement of self-consciousness or self-reflection within this original unity caused it to shatter into fragments. Cascades of spiritual beings came into successive existence, and ended with the appearance of the Demiurge and the creation of the material world. Gnostics are human beings who are rediscovering their true identity in connection with the Pleroma. They are shards of light from the celestial creation, trapped in material bodies, and exiled from their true home. By discovering who they really are, and from whence they have come, they can be set free and return home. To do this, one has to free oneself from the constraints of the material realm. Jesus is the supreme Gnostic teacher, a messenger come to awaken us to our true identity and bring us back. 'Blessed are you,' says Jesus to Judas in the Gospel of Judas, 'because you will set me free from the man who clothes me.' The 'man who clothes me' is not Jesus's tailor, but the earthly body within which his true self is imprisoned. In betraying Jesus to death on the cross, Judas will do him the greatest possible service, for Jesus will then finally be set free from the flesh. This is a good example of a general point. The Gnostics did not simply read their own texts *rather than* what were to become the canonical texts of Christian Scripture; they read the Gospels of Thomas or Judas *as well as* the Gospels of Luke or John; and the point of the special writings is often to draw out the 'true meaning' of what the commonly read texts say. The mainstream Gospels tell us that Judas betrayed Jesus. To the uninitiated, this seems supremely culpable. The reader of the Gospel of Thomas is given the true, deeper meaning of Judas's action. Genesis 1—2 and the Fourth Gospel especially held out the promise of gnosticizing interpretations, and it is no accident that the first known commentary on John's Gospel was written by a pupil of Valentinus, named Herakleon.

The opponents of the Gnostics responded in three ways. First, they accused the Gnostics of not caring what they did with their bodies, and engaging in all kinds of immoral bodily behaviour as if it did not matter. There may indeed have been some Gnostics who really did think that, if the body were only a fleshly envelope for the real self within, it did not matter what they did with it – and the members of any secret and religiously intense group are especially open to sexual exploitation – but on the whole these lurid accusations of Gnostic orgies are unfair. Gnostic ethics are much more likely to be fiercely ascetical. The body is to be subjugated, and its appetites – for food, or sleep, or sex – are to be resisted. The divine spark has to be freed from the tyranny of the clay that encloses it.

The second response is more substantial and has become a fundamental part of Christian teaching. The mainstream Church would have nothing to do with demiurges and low-ranking creator-gods. There is only one creator of everything that there is, and that is God; the maker of our world is the maker of all that is made, terrestrial and celestial, and it comes into existence because of God's good will. However much modern cosmology or evolutionary biology may challenge theologians to restate what it means to claim that the world is made by God, or in what way God makes the world, God is always, as the Nicene Creed puts it, the 'Maker of heaven and earth, And of all things visible and invisible' (p. 10). This insistence was sharpened by a controversy that also took place in the second half of the second century in connection with Marcion, who gave his name to Marcionism (see Chapter 7), who was not a Gnostic, but whose teaching about creation coincided with some Gnostic ideas. Marcion drew a sharp distinction between the God of the Old Testament – the God who creates the world in Genesis 1—2, and who goes on to show himself (in Marcion's view) a hateful God of anger and vengeance – and the God of the New Testament – the God of love whom Jesus proclaims, and of whom the human race was wholly ignorant before Jesus came to reveal him. In response, the Christian Church again insisted that the loving Father proclaimed by Jesus is the same as the creator of the world. The material world is in itself fundamentally good and the radical Gnostic depreciation of the body is mistaken. Indeed, as Christians went on to reflect more deeply on God's redemptive work in Jesus Christ, they came to see more and more clearly the essential goodness of the created world. Christ came to redeem the world, and he did so by entering into creation himself, being born as a child in Bethlehem: 'The Word became flesh and dwelt among us' (John 1.14). Human flesh in which the Word has chosen to dwell cannot be essentially bad.

The third response was also directed towards both Marcion and the Gnostics. Marcion would not allow that any of what he was possibly the first to call the Old Testament could be read as Christian Scripture. It was about the hateful creator-god. And since the New Testament writings often quote the Old Testament, and indeed present Jesus as the fulfilment of its prophecies, Marcion found that he had to cut out much of the New Testament as well. His Christian Bible (as noted in Chapter 7) was a slender collection: just Luke's Gospel, and an edited version of the letters of Paul. The Gnostic teachers went in the opposite direction. They not only read those books commonly read in the churches, but gave authority – generally even greater authority – to the Gospels of Philip, or Thomas, or Mary, and to numerous other collections of sayings and stories attached to Jesus or to one of the apostles. What was the genuine teaching of Jesus, as handed down through the apostles, according to the Church? It was a lot more than you could find in Marcion's slim collection and a lot less than you could find in the Gnostic collection. The simultaneous operation of these two forces is the main reason for the emergence, between the mid-second and the mid-third centuries, of a reasonably definitive canon of Christian Scripture. This canon still had rough edges, which went on to be polished in the fourth century and later, but the selection of texts in the Christian Bible as we know it was essentially determined by the middle of the third century. This complex process, of the Church's making up its collective mind about which books should or should not be read as Christian Scripture, cannot be reduced to the simple decision of this or that council of bishops. In particular, the Council of Nicea in 325 had little or nothing to do with it, despite the claim to the contrary in Dan Brown's *The Da Vinci Code*. The process began much earlier and ended later. But Dan Brown's book alerts us to the continuing attraction of the Gnostic idea that the official Scriptures of the Church are not enough for finding the truth about Jesus. The real truth is allegedly to be found in unofficial books, which the Church does not want you to read, and has energetically tried to suppress. Apart from its gross simplification of the historical process by which the canon of Christian Scripture came into existence, this stands the true dynamic exactly on its head. It was the Gnostics who wanted to keep the truth about Jesus hidden. One had to be worthy to be initiated into the real truth about him. Pearls were not to be cast before swine; heavenly secrets were not for earth-bound people. The mainstream Church, by contrast, insisted that the truth about Jesus was to be found in the Scriptures that were openly read in church. Gnostic scriptures were indeed actively suppressed by bishops like Athanasius, not because they contained truths which he wanted to conceal, but because he thought they contained falsehoods which would do people harm. We may deplore, from the perspective of twenty-first-century religious tolerance, the active suppression of heterodox literature (literature that fails to conform with orthodox beliefs), but we should not confuse the motive of the bishop doing the suppressing, or suppose that there was nothing more to his exercise of power than the desire to hold on to it. The appropriate contemporary response to the revival of the idea that the truth about Jesus is to be found through the Gnostic texts, amazingly recovered from the past by chance and patient scholarship, is not to stop people reading them, but to encourage them back to the more profound, coherent and hopeful account of creation (by God) and redemption (by and in Christ) which is to be found in the canonical Gospels, the letters of Paul, and the other writings of the Christian Bible.

Whether the elaborate Gnostic cosmogonies (theories about the origin of the universe) still have their present-day followers is harder to determine. The importance of female principles (like Faith or Wisdom) in some Gnostic systems has made them attractive when so much theology is conducted in exclusively male God-language, but it is not necessary to enter the Gnostic world to explore, for example, divine Wisdom as a way of approaching God's work in Christ. The identification of the Wisdom of Old Testament tradition, personified as female in Proverbs 8 and elsewhere, is normal in early Christian thought, and the development of 'Wisdom Christology' has been an important feature of recent Christian thought. It is when a dualism of male and female principles is made absolute and projected onto the divine that things go wrong. This kind of dualism is found in some Gnostic writings, as well as in other religious systems. In *The Da Vinci Code* and similar modern writings, it is linked to the idea that Jesus was married to Mary Magdalene. This tradition was found only in a very small part of the Gnostic spectrum, the majority of which was concerned to emphasize Jesus's distance from the flesh and all that it entails. The canonical Gospels, meanwhile, show us a Jesus who is able to give immediate and intensely loving attention to an enormous variety of people who cross his path, in a way that is characteristic of those who do not concentrate their love on a spouse or children of their own.

The elaborate Gnostic cosmogonies may have only distant echoes in the modern world, but what of the fundamental idea that underlay them, that redemption from all that is alienated and wrong in our human condition comes through a process of knowing – knowing who we truly are, and knowing whence we have come? The importance of knowledge-as-redemption comes out especially clearly when the Gnostic literature of late antiquity is read alongside the magical texts that have survived from the same period. There are some striking similarities. The complex hierarchies of heavenly beings are similar; they have the same elaborate names, often derived from fragments of Hebrew; and both come from an insecure world in which life-expectancy was short and many struggled to keep themselves above the level of subsistence. But there are significant differences too. The magicians sought knowledge of the heavenly hierarchies in order to manipulate them on their clients' behalf. In a world without proper dentistry, powerful forces have to be summoned to deal with toothache (which appears with remarkable frequency in the Greek Magical Papyri). The Gnostics, on the other hand, sought knowledge of the heavenly hierarchies not in order to manipulate them, but so that the soul, the fragile spark of light, might escape from toothache and all the limitations of its bodily prison, and thread its way back to its true home in a spiritual realm.

Both the knowledge of the magicians and the knowledge of the Gnostics are different from the knowledge of orthodox Christians. Christians seek knowledge of the divine neither in order to manipulate it nor in order to escape the bodily realm. Christians are those who know themselves to have been redeemed in Christ and transformed by incorporation into his death and resurrection and by his gift of the Holy Spirit.

Is there a modern-day version of Gnosticism that Christians should seek to avoid? A psychotherapy which suggested that the knowledge that we gain of ourselves in the psychotherapeutic relationship is itself what makes us whole human beings would perhaps be a genuine Gnosticism in a contemporary form. It would have substituted self-knowledge for God's redemptive initiative in Christ. For Gnostics, ancient and modern, Jesus redeems us by teaching, by helping us to understand ourselves (which is why Gnostic Gospels like that of Thomas consist almost entirely of sayings). For the Church, Jesus is not just a teacher, but the Christ, the risen Lord, the Word made flesh for the world's redemption.

11

The heresy of the Free Spirit:
Are there two kinds of Christian,
those with divine wills
and those with human wills?

DENYS TURNER

━━━━━◆━━━━━

What is the heresy of the Free Spirit?

The heresy of the Free Spirit asserts that Christian perfection consists in the annihilation of one's will and its replacement by God's will. It is associated with Marguerite Porete, author of *The Mirror of Simple Souls*, who was burned at the stake in 1310 for continuing to circulate copies of a book already ruled to be heretical. By suggesting that the human will could be replaced by the divine will, the heresy of the Free Spirit revisits the error of Apollinarianism (see Chapter 2), and, by implying that there are two tiers of Christian discipleship, it is reminiscent of the error of the Donatists (see Chapter 8). It was condemned at the Council of Vienne in 1312.

*   *   *

Key Scriptures

'You, therefore, must be perfect, as your heavenly Father is perfect.' (Matthew 5.48)

It is no longer I who live, but Christ who lives in me. (Galatians 2.20b)

*   *   *

Forty years ago I met a canonized saint. Of course, he wasn't canonized at the time. That was done early in 2002 by Pope John Paul II, who was apparently by some measure more prolific in awarding the holiness laureate than all of his predecessors combined. Alas, one suspects a similar degree of grade-inflation in the holiness stakes to that one has witnessed in certain school examinations and some university degrees over much the same period: a sort of 'dumbing down', a lowering of the thresholds. And my own impression of the man – based partly upon personal and very brief acquaintance with him, but mainly upon reflection on his record since then (he died about ten years after I met him) – was of distinctly second-grade elements mixed in with elements of pure genius. Ambiguous.

The saint in question was Josemaría Escrivá de Balaguer, but the point here is about ambiguity; ambiguity at many levels, but above all the ambiguity of lives – of all lives but especially of those geniuses of the spirit, those (they are rarely in fact canonized) who have responded with more than common radicalness to that command of Jesus quoted at the head of this chapter: 'You, therefore, must be perfect, as your heavenly Father is perfect' (Matthew 5.48).

Such people, being in one way or another 'originals', are very hard to read. They are ambiguous. They do not quite fit our prior models, and it is not just that they are a fraction too big for them: rather, they transform the very models they are measured by. So at first they startle. I often say to students: please, never try getting Plato into your heads. Plato's mind is vast, and yours and mine are small. Getting Plato in your head is bound to diminish his and it will cause headaches in yours. Try to get your head into Plato's and there your mind has room to roam and explore in uncharted, limitless, territory. Saints are a little like that. Our models constrain, and saints' lives transgress their boundaries.

And as for heresies, they too are always, at least at first, ambiguous. At first you are unsure about them, for they flirt with given boundaries of doctrine or of practice, and it can be hard to tell whether they do so creatively or destructively. In fact, it is my guess that rarely is it their being perceived to be plainly wrong which troubles the Church about heresies; it is rather their refusal to be plain; it is their unnerving ambiguity which seems subversive, with heresy as with holiness. And what is distinctive about the 'Heresy of the Free Spirit' is the intensified character of its ambiguities. For it is ambiguous, as heresies are, about a thing which is itself ambiguous, about holiness, for if this heresy be a heresy, then that, holiness, is what it is a heresy about. As you might say, what this heresy offers is an ambiguous reading of that text from Matthew: 'You [. . .] must be perfect as your heavenly Father is perfect' (5.48) And in the early fourteenth century the 'Free Spirit' heresy was associated with a young French woman named Marguerite Porete.

Little is known about Marguerite Porete. There is but one certain date: she was burned at the stake on 1 June 1310 at the Place des Graves in Paris for refusing to suppress her manu-script, now known in English as *The Mirror of Simple Souls*. One supposes that she must have achieved some degree of circula-tion for her work before her execution, and that not all the copies of the manuscript were burned with her, for, no more than thirty years after her execution, her text is found circulating widely, not only in her vernacular Old French original, but also in many an Italian manuscript, in a Latin version, presumably made by William Humbert, the inquisitor who tried her, and by the end of the fourteenth century there is a Middle English version (which is used to supply a few missing sections of her original text). But by then the work is no longer suspect, and some say this is because it is no longer attributed to Marguerite herself, a mere woman, but is now ascribed to an anonym-ous author, presumed to be male. Indeed, there is a modern English rendition of the Middle English text of the *Mirror* pub-lished in London in 1927 with the imprimatur of the Cardinal

Archbishop of Westminster and attributed to 'An anonymous Carthusian monk'. It was not until 1946 that it was finally established that the *Mirror* was after all the missing text for which Marguerite was tried and burned on a charge of heresy.

And the heresy she was charged with was the heresy of the 'Free Spirit' – or at least that is how it was named when it was condemned at the Council of Vienne a year or two after Marguerite's death; several of the condemned propositions in the Bull *Ad Nostrum* reflected her teaching, if not verbatim, then at least in substance. Nonetheless, Malcolm D. Lambert and Robert E. Lerner, the two leading authorities on medieval heresy, are agreed that it was the Council of Vienne which helped create heretics to match the Bull. It is certainly true that no known author in the Middle Ages espouses just that compendious collection of propositions condemned at that Council, not even Marguerite herself. For although some of the propositions condemned as 'Free Spirit heresy' by Vienne reflect her teaching, patently the citations are one-sidedly selective and it is only in this extracted form that they are plainly heretical. So it is at least true to say that Vienne *compiled* the heresy to match its condemnations, even if it is less than true to say that it *created* it.

Heresy hunters and inquisitors need combustible substance, hard and literal dry errors; damp ambiguities make poor tinder. But it is the ambiguities which truly threaten authorities, because authorities need the fixity of boundary which ambiguities toy with. So, if you are an inquisitor, the first step is to organize the heresy into condemnable form, to disambiguate it. Yet this work of Marguerite's resists such easy précis. It is like shot-silk; its hue ever changes with the angle of refraction. Marguerite is a conscious flirt doctrinally: she eludes the very advances she elicits. So all the frustrated inquisitors can do is make her mind up for her, and then, with due ceremony, dump her.

The Mirror takes the form of a debate mainly between three personifications, the Soul, Love and Reason. The Soul seeks the love of God, Love answers sympathetically, Reason poses objections to Love's answers. In the course of this three-way debate, Love draws out a distinction, which was bound to be considered provoking, between 'Holy Church the Great' and 'Holy Church the Less', the former consisting in the community of those souls who are 'unencumbered', or 'annihilated', or 'perfected' in the service of Love, while to Holy Church the Less belong those who live in the service of Reason.

Now the precise nature of this distinction is less than clear in itself, though Marguerite does not cheapen it by accusing the 'lesser' Church of corruption; lesser souls are good Christians, she says, they live by the virtues, the conventional practices of prayer, of asceticism and of the sacraments. But the followers of Holy Church the Great have reached a higher condition of spiritual achievement, superior to any which can be reached by those conventional means, a condition of complete 'annihilation' and abandonment to love: they live in 'freedom of spirit'. These souls have no will of their own, they need no reasons of their own, for – their own wills having been displaced by God's uncreated will – they live entirely by means of the divine will, and so live, as she puts it, 'without a why' of their own. So the distinction is, in the first instance, a moral distinction between two qualities or levels of achievement of Christian life.

What was less clear, troublingly no doubt to Church authorities, was the bearing that this moral distinction had on the actual Church as institution. Was Marguerite saying that the annihilated soul had no need of the institutional Church, of its prayers and sacraments, its ascetical disciplines and charitable works? She answers 'Yes' and 'No'. The 'free spirit' does not depend on them. But neither may she abandon them. She is 'free' of them only in the sense that she is able to use them freely. Here, perhaps more than anywhere, Marguerite seems to taunt Reason with ambiguity: if she concedes that those who live by virtue, the sacraments and the ordinary means of grace and good works, that is to say, by Reason, can be saved and are good, she is at best condescending to the claims of Holy Church the Less and at worst appears to doubt whether it has any future. And what holds for Holy Church the Less holds for all the everyday means of holiness which the Church provides, indeed of all ordinary morality, of the virtues of the good life themselves.

And it is this sort of statement which gets her into trouble – these are her own words:

> *Love*: Once a soul has reached this state [of annihilation], she can say to the virtues: 'I have no further need of you, now I have served you all this time.'
>
> *The Soul*: I agree, dear Love. I was their servant, but your kind courtesy has set me free from enslavement to them. Virtues, I leave you behind forever! My heart is now freer and more at peace than it has ever been. It was hard work being your servant; that I know well. For a time I put my heart inseparably into your service and you knew it: I was completely given over to you, therefore then I was your slave, but now I am released, and I wonder how I was able to escape.
>
> *Love*: This soul knows no care, has neither shame nor honour, neither poverty nor riches, neither joy nor sorrow, neither love nor hate, neither hell nor heaven.
>
> *Reason*: For God's sake, Love, what are you saying?
>
> *Love*: What I mean can be understood only by those to whom God has given understanding and by none other; it is not taught by Scripture, nor can human reason work it out . . . It is a gift received from the Most High, in whom all knowing leads to loss of understanding . . . So this soul that has become nothing possesses all and possesses nothing, knows all and knows nothing, wills everything and wills nothing . . . [and this is] because . . . it is not the soul's will that wills, but God's will willing in her; the soul does not rest in love as if led to it by any desires of her own. Rather, love rests in her, takes over her

will, and has her will of her. So now love can work in the soul without the soul's will, and the soul will be freed from all cares. (*Mirror* 6.1–7.26)

It is very easy to see how you could read Marguerite in a plainly antinomian and spiritually élite sense. To her inquisitors it is as if she were saying, 'Be you perfect, and you don't need the virtues, the sacraments, the Church . . . which are good enough for the run-of-the-mill Christians of Holy Church the Less, but not for "free spirits".' For Marguerite, it seems, good enough is not good enough; did not Christ say, 'You must be *perfect*'? Yet how else could it seem to her accusers than that her 'perfect' is the enemy of their 'good'?

But just as you think that that is what she is saying, the angle of refraction shifts. It is not, she says, that the perfected soul does not act virtuously, or receive the sacraments. She does. For the 'free spirit' does all that virtue commands, but not as commanded; she does as freedom what the merely virtuous person does as obligation. She is perfected in love; and because a perfect lover does in freedom what the imperfect lover does as duty, she is 'free' of the virtues in that sense alone in which she does nothing out of need. She needs nothing, because she has no will of her own out of which to experience any need.

Nor is she alone in saying such things. Perhaps as little as five years after Marguerite's execution, Meister Eckhart took up this theme of total abandonment to love and he repeats her phrase: such a soul 'lives without a why', he says; seeks God without attachment to means or mediation of any kind, and does not even know or need a 'way' to God: for, as he says, 'those who seek God in ways will find ways and lose God, who in ways is hidden'. And John of the Cross says much the same, 'the land of the spirit is a land without ways'.

So, if they get away with it, why not Marguerite? Why did she seem so subversive, why did her ambiguity so threaten? Why did the Church need to reduce Marguerite's subtle ambiguities to a trite, and so condemnable, plainness? Because ambiguity challenges the clear contours of boundary, and so challenges the authority which polices them. Because Marguerite's 'free spirit' does all that the Church commands she eludes easy moral condemnation – no libertine she. But because in her freedom of spirit she does not need the Church to command her, the Church is threatened in its self-conception as the necessary means of holiness. Marguerite does not need the Church, such is her freedom of spirit. But Holy Church the Less needs to be needed, for that, in Marguerite's eyes, is what makes it to be the 'Lesser' Church that it is. It feeds off a spiritual dependence which it first creates, and then reinforces, in its members. For her, Holy Church the Less is thus constituted by a self-perpetuating cycle of mutual neediness. Marguerite, however, is 'unencumbered' by any such need. Because she has no will of her own, she wants nothing of her own. Because she wants nothing of her own, she needs nothing. Because she needs nothing, she owes nothing. And in that 'nothingness' of her self she is entirely free, an 'unencumbered' soul.

Maybe it is in that way that Marguerite reads Paul's exclamation, also quoted at the head of this chapter, that it was no longer he who lived, but Christ who lived in him. But Paul needed the Church – even though he was holy he needed support from those around him. And might one not fairly ask of Marguerite: free of all 'need' she may very well be, but does not freedom as she conceives of it also amount to a freedom from all mutuality, all relationship? The one thing that can be asked of her 'Holy Church the Great', great and holy as it might be, is how can it be in any way a church if its members have no need – at least of one another?

I end with just this thought, since you will want to know why we should hear of this heresy today, and of how we might avoid it. Today too, unchurched 'spiritualities' abound, and, because they attract many, they still have the capacity to make 'churched' Christians uneasy. Might not such Christians today legitimately share the fears, if not the inquisitorial methods, of William Humbert who conducted Marguerite's trial in Paris? And might not those Christians who have been brought up in a legacy of an impossible Christian 'perfectionism' (they are not a few) have reason to exorcise the ghosts of it which haunt their unhappiness of conscience, seeing therein only two possibilities: a striving for an unachievable 'total' freedom of spirit, and the guilt-ridden sense of the failure to have achieved it?

And as for Marguerite's 'Holy Church the Great', is there not in her conception of it a lurking, spiritual élitism, a recrudescence of the Donatist mentality which Ben Quash discussed in Chapter 8? Not long ago a student came to me saying that she was taking instruction to be received into the Roman Catholic Church. Sensing that she had a somewhat idealized picture of my Church, I said to her, in a sort of inverted Marxian spirit (though of the sub-class Groucho) that I couldn't bear to be a member of a Church which wasn't corrupt enough to want me as a member of it. I suppose I meant that there is no one who is without at least one need: the need to be forgiven. And there is no one who does not need the community of those who know only of their need for that forgiveness, for it is only in our receiving it from others that we have any power to return it. And if there is one heresy that the Church needs to exclude, it is the heresy of spiritual exclusiveness. True 'freedom of spirit', the freedom of spirit which is truly 'perfect', lies in a perfect receptiveness to that fact of our having been forgiven. And a Church founded on and living in the means of that forgiveness might indeed be a 'Holy Church' of 'the Less'; but it would be a Church worth dying for. As Jesus did, who founded his Church on the cross in the act of forgiving all murderers, including, one thinks, even Marguerite's. And Marguerite herself too. All of them and us together in that messy chaos, as ambiguous as it is vibrant, which is the one true Church, founded in the name of the Father, the Son, and the Holy Spirit.

12

Biblical Trinitarianism: The purpose of being orthodox

JANET MARTIN SOSKICE

———◆•◆•◆———

What is Biblical Trinitarianism?

The doctrine and worship of the Trinity are the ends to which avoidance of heresy is intended to lead. But orthodox doctrine may sometimes be defended, and orthodox worship may sometimes be encouraged, on grounds which are themselves of questionable orthodoxy. The 'Johannine Comma', an early medieval interpolation into Scripture, designed to bolster the evidence for the Trinity, possibly in the face of Arian persecution, is one such example. Scholars believe that it had become worked into copies of the Latin Bible, the *Vulgate*, around the year 800, and from there spread into English and other versions. It was removed from the updated edition of the *Vulgate*, published in 1979 as a result of the Second Vatican Council. The doctrine of the Trinity was developed by the Church in the first five centuries, relying on scriptures which were deemed to be traceable to the teachings or writings of the first apostles (for example, Matthew 28.19; Luke 3.22; Luke 9.28–36; John 1.14).

*   *   *

Key Scriptures

Who is he that overcometh the world, but he that believeth that Jesus is the Son of God? This is he that came by water and blood, even Jesus Christ; not by water only, but by water and blood. And it is the Spirit that beareth witness, because the Spirit is the truth. For there are three that bear record in heaven, the Father, the Word, and the Holy Ghost: and these three are one. And there are three that bear witness in earth, the spirit, and the water, and the blood: and these three agree in one. If we receive the witness of men, the witness of God is greater: for this is the witness of God which he hath testified of his Son. (1 John 5.5–9, King James Version)

Jesus took with him Peter and John and James, and went up on the mountain to pray. And as he was praying, the appearance of his countenance was altered, and his raiment became dazzling white. And behold, two men talked with him, Moses and Elijah, who appeared in glory and spoke of his departure, which he was to accomplish at Jerusalem. Now Peter and those who were with him were heavy with sleep but kept awake, and they saw his glory and the two men who stood with him. And as the men were parting from him, Peter said to Jesus, 'Master, it is well that we are here; let us make three booths, one for you and one for Moses and one for Elijah' – not knowing what he said. As he said this, a cloud came and overshadowed them; and they were afraid as they entered the cloud. And a voice came out of the cloud, saying, 'This is my Son, my Chosen; listen to him!' And when the voice had spoken, Jesus was found alone. And they kept silence and told no one in those days anything of what they had seen. (Luke 9.28–36)

*   *   *

Probably all of us have wondered exactly what it means to believe in the Trinity and have asked ourselves if we really do, and if so, why we do. Even the clergy notoriously struggle to get a visiting preacher for Trinity Sunday – it's a difficult subject to talk about. John Henry Newman's great blast of faith from *The Dream of Gerontius*, sung now to a swaggering hymn tune – 'Firmly I believe and truly, God is Three and God is One' – always sounds slightly strained. If you do believe so very firmly and truly, why go on about it like this? My purpose in this

123

chapter is not to tell you how to avoid a heresy, but to restate a positive orthodoxy – Trinitarian faith – although not without unsettling you a little first. Let us begin by rereading some of the verses from the first epistle of John which are quoted at the head of this chapter: '*For there are three that bear record in heaven, the Father, the Word, and the Holy Ghost; and these three are one*, and there are three that testify on earth, the Spirit, the water, and the blood, and these three agree in one. If we receive the witness of men, the witness of God is greater: for this is the witness of God which he hath testified of his Son' (1 John 5.7–9).

You may be forgiven for not recognizing the words I have put in italics for the simple reason that, if you are best familiar with modern translations of the Bible, these words are not there. Some of us know the scriptures through singing them; people with a choral background may well recognize these words from settings of church music – from Monteverdi's Vespers, for instance. Right up through the nineteenth century these words were cherished as Holy Writ, almost the only passage in the New Testament with an unequivocal confession of the doctrine of the Trinity.

The trouble is that there is no evidence for this verse in any early Greek manuscripts of the Bible (prior to 1200) and they only appear in Latin Bibles from about the year 800, from which time they gradually became widespread.

All this prompted quite a crisis for Erasmus, the first lecturer in Greek at the University of Cambridge, but more famous for producing, in 1516, the first *printed* Greek New Testament. Reformers like Erasmus and John Calvin wanted to go back behind the Latin of the medieval Bible to the original Greek. *Ad fontes!* ('To the well-spring!') was their cry. They wanted to do so because they wanted a faith pure, honest and attentive to the actual words of the apostles, and not to the medieval glosses and accretions of the Church, but also because they were humanists and a generation of extraordinarily gifted linguists and textual scholars. Honesty to the Word of God was of the essence to their reforming faith.

Prior to the development of the printing press in the early modern period, Bibles did not just lie around for anyone to pick up at will, and especially not Greek New Testaments. All copies of the Bible were handwritten and all liable to scribal error or deliberate scribal emendations and interpolations. There were Greek manuscripts of the New Testament all over Europe and the Middle East, in libraries, in monasteries, in royal collections and the Vatican. These manuscripts varied considerably in age and quality, and even in which books of the New Testament they contained. Many, for instance, lacked the book of Revelation entirely.

Erasmus put his Greek New Testament together in haste, relying for the most part on those manuscripts he could lay hands on in Basle. But even then he could see that the Trinitarian invocation of the First Letter of John (5.7) – 'For there are three that bear record in heaven, the Father, the Word, and the Holy Ghost; and these three are one' (a passage which became known as the 'Johannine Comma') – was almost without doubt a gloss inserted at some stage by a pious scribe and then passed down to later copies as original. When Erasmus first published his Greek New Testament he left these words out.

There was consternation in the learned community, Reformed and Catholic, and in the third edition of his Greek New Testament, published in 1522, Erasmus reinserted the dubious verses. These in turn passed down into most vernacular translations of the Bible, including the King James Version of 1611, historically the most influential version in the English-speaking world.

The doctrine of the Trinity had some close moments in the seventeenth and eighteenth centuries, not least in Erasmus's Cambridge, where Trinitarian controversies continued to rage; for example, Newton, based at Trinity College, was famously not a Trinitarian. This was not because of the Johannine Comma, whose dubious origins had largely been forgotten, but because the doctrine seemed, to a biblically formed Church, insufficiently scriptural.

All knew that the developed doctrine was hammered out in the third and fourth centuries by means of terms like *ousia* and *hypostasis* – terms from Greek metaphysics, not the New Testament scriptures, both of which mean something like 'essence' or 'substance'. 'I wish I could toss the lot of them,' Calvin had said, commenting on these non-scriptural origins, 'except that they are so useful in ferreting out the heretics!'

The Johannine Comma lay ticking like a time-bomb all through this period, while internecine disputes pushed some Christian groups to make more and more extreme claims for Scripture – that it was fully inspired, wholly inspired, totally inerrant in substance, even fully inspired in every word, conjugation and piece of punctuation. Calvin, with his knowledge of texts and manuscripts, could never have made the claims of some eighteenth-century Calvinists.

By the nineteenth century, crisis was unavoidable: the Johannine Comma was without scholarly doubt a medieval interpolation and it began to disappear from new editions and translations of the Bible. The interesting thing about this crisis over the text of Scripture (of which this text from 1 John was only one example) was that it was not clear, to a fundamentally evangelical Britain, which side could most truly claim to be clinging fast to the authority of Scripture. Was it those who stood by the Old Bible, a book cherished word by individual word by English-speaking Christians for two hundred years, or was it those who honestly said that this clearly medieval interpolation should be eradicated in a new translation? Ironically, the text of 1 John enhances this difficulty since this is the Epistle that states, in the verse immediately following the passage quoted above, that 'If we receive the witness of men, the witness of God is greater' (1 John 5.9). But the question precisely was, which is the witness of God and which the witness of men?

In the nineteenth century, congregations and denominations were torn apart by such questions, especially those like the Presbyterians who aligned themselves closely to Scripture and held strong views of inerrancy. For it wasn't sceptics or infidels who were rocking the craft of faith at the time but devout men, products of Scottish manses, like the distinguished Semitic scholar William Robertson Smith, who – propelled from his Aberdeen Chair after a heresy trial in the 1880s for denying that Moses wrote the Pentateuch, the first five books of the Bible – then moved to Cambridge as Professor of Arabic. Smith was an evangelical Christian who did not ever doubt that the Old Testament was the inspired testimony to God's self-disclosure to Israel, but he thought this disclosure was gradual, and just in so far as it was revelation to human beings that it would be affected by their customs and history, their kinship patterns and their figures of speech. (Robertson Smith's work was not only decisive in biblical studies, but influential also on Sigmund Freud, Emile Durkheim, and Marcel Mauss. Smith was Freud's favourite writer on religion.)

Some lost their faith over such questions. George Eliot, who translated works of German higher criticism for an intellectually innocent British population, was one. But many others, really the majority, delighted in the new light shed upon the Gospels. And nor was the doctrine of the Trinity left desolate.

A spasm of 'isms' surrounds the formal history of the doctrine of the Trinity – some of which, such as Arianism and Docetism, have already been discussed (see Chapters 1 and 2) – and these are important matters of study for future ministers and priests who need to understand the history and the development of Christian doctrine. For ordinary people, however, the important thing is to realize that, despite its grand historical wrappings, the doctrine of the Trinity is eminently practical.

The doctrine of the Trinity is the easiest thing about Christian teaching and also – if this doesn't seem too improbable – the means by which Christianity stays closest to its Jewish roots. Of course, if we were to stop a few Christians in the street and ask them, 'Do you believe in the doctrine of the Trinity?', we would probably get stammers and blushes. This is because we would be asking the wrong question. We should rather be asking, 'Can you confess the Creeds?' For when we recite the Apostles' Creed (p. 10) or the Nicene Creed (pp. 10–11) and confess our belief in God as Father, Son and Holy Spirit, we find that the Creeds do not add the further clause – 'and we also believe in the Trinity' – because to confess belief in one God, Father, Son and Holy Spirit, is to confess the Trinity, or better, it is to be a Trinitarian Christian.

The doctrine of the Trinity was formulated in the early Church not as abstruse metaphysical meanderings but in response to the needs of street-level Christianity. In the early days of the Church, market traders along the Bosphorus were arguing because the Christians were praying to Jesus, and praying at the same time to the one he called 'Father'. In the antique world it would be natural for Jews and pagans alike to assume that these Christians were polytheists – that their Jesus was a lesser God, a servant to the High God. But the orthodox Christians denied this was what they believed. They insisted that, like the Jews, they worshipped the one God. Their startling claim was that Jesus was not a demi-god or a semi-god, but very God. God incarnate.

Even if the scriptures never use the word 'Trinity', the very earliest of the Christian scriptural writings – the letters of Paul – make bold claims for Jesus, some of whose implications have been fully understood only with work done by Jewish and Christian scholars over the past twenty or thirty years. For instance, in 2 Corinthians 4.6, Paul identifies Jesus with the God who said 'Let light shine out of darkness' and with the divine glory. Paul applies titles to Jesus which a devout Jew of his day would have applied only to the God who created heaven and earth.

When the author of 1 John tells his Christian audience that, by believing 'in the name of the Son of God' they may know that they have 'eternal life' (1 John 5.13), he echoes John's Gospel (20.31), where believers are promised 'life in his name'. For a Jew 'to call upon the name of the Lord' is to pray, and the only Name that gives salvation is that of the One who made heaven and earth. It seems clear that the early Christians believed Jesus to be the Messiah, the very presence of God among them. And this is what Christians believe today, too. Every Easter and every Sunday we celebrate the risen Christ, present with us.

And this brings me to Luke's account of the Transfiguration (Luke 9.28–36, quoted at the head of this chapter). Jesus goes with Peter, John and James up a mountain to pray. As he does so his clothing becomes a dazzling white and the disciples see Moses and Elijah talking to him. Luke even tells us what they were talking about – his departure to Jerusalem and by implication his death. For 'departure' Luke uses the word 'exodus' – Moses, Elijah and Jesus are talking about the Lord's *exodus*.

The normal biblical moment chosen by artists in the Western tradition to illustrate the doctrine of the Trinity is the baptism of Jesus by John: we have the sky torn apart, the conveniently explicit dove descending, and the voice from heaven which says, '*Thou* art my beloved Son; with thee I am well pleased' (Luke 3.22).

The Eastern Church has a preference for the Transfiguration. The heavens are again rent by a voice saying, this time not to Jesus but to his disciples, '*This* is my Son, my Chosen, listen to him!' The dove is not present, but instead Jesus and his garments shine with an uncreated light, the very Shekinah of God.

Western Bible commentaries tend to say, rather woodenly, that Moses and Elijah appear alongside Jesus at the Transfiguration because they represent the Law and the Prophets. But the Eastern Church sees Luke as reminding us of another mountain top, that of Sinai, for Moses and Elijah are *just those two prophets* who experienced theophanies on Mount Sinai: Moses in the burning bush (Exodus 3.1–15) and Elijah in the whispered voice (1 Kings 19.8–13). These two now appear with Jesus, the new Israel, and talk to him of his 'going out'.

We read in the book of Exodus that, when Moses spoke with the Lord on Sinai, his face became so bright with the reflected divine glory that he had to veil his face on his descent so as not to dazzle the other Israelites. In the Transfiguration, Christ himself is the very Light through which all things are made, the Light which has come into the world and 'tabernacles' (or dwells among) us – God's Shekinah.

We therefore do not need the Johannine Comma, the work of some well-meaning medieval scribe, to be assured of the scriptural basis for the doctrine of the Trinity. Although it may have taken several Councils and several centuries for the Church to formulate the doctrine, it is by no means a late invention, but can be found in the New Testament itself. For as John says, 'And the Word became flesh and dwelt among us, full of grace and truth; we have beheld his glory, glory as of the only Son from the Father' (John 1.14). No clearer statement of the Trinity is needed than this, for the Transfigured Christ is God-with-us, the beloved Son of the Father, ablaze with the Light of the Spirit.

Epilogue

MICHAEL WARD

———◆◆◆———

The first eleven chapters of this book have shown how important it is to avoid heresy. Heretical beliefs, however superficially attractive, are always dangerous in the long-run, both
to ourselves and to others. The link which Angela Tilby made
in Chapter 7 between Marcionist attitudes and anti-Semitism
is only the most obvious of the connections drawn in these pages
between the errors of the heretics and all-too-palpable (and all-
too-contemporary) ills. Allison's book, *The Cruelty of Heresy*,
recommended in the 'For further reading' section (p. 146),
pursues this theme in an interesting way.

The twelfth chapter turned our focus away from heresy to
orthodoxy and did so for a very good reason: orthodoxy is more
than the sum of its avoidances. It is something of a fashion, in
our pain-denying and litigious Western societies, to be risk-averse,
to wrap ourselves up ever more tightly in a 'health-and-safety'
mentality and lead a life characterized largely by evasions
and precautions. But Christian orthodoxy is not a product of
that mentality and is not merely a negative condition; the
doughnut is what describes the hole, not vice versa. The positive content of Christian faith is the more excellent way to live
life as a member of the Church, and that positive content
consists of God's glory and our enjoyment of it. We have had
occasion several times in this book to refer to *Against Heresies*,
the classic heresy-hunting work of Irenaeus, but it is worth
emphasizing what is perhaps the most famous line from that
work, which has already been quoted in Chapter 7, namely: *Gloria
Dei vivens homo* – 'the glory of God is a human being fully alive'
(IV. 20. 7). These words of Irenaeus are but a gloss on Jesus's

saying in the Gospel of John (10.10): 'I came that they may have life, and have it abundantly.' Living life in all its fullness is the surest way to proceed. Knowing where you're heading, knowing why you're going, desiring your destination, carrying a map in your hand, stopping frequently and gratefully for food, and having the company of fellow walkers ahead of you, behind you, and on either hand, not to mention a great cloud of witnesses above you – that is the safest and happiest kind of pilgrimage. Sidestepping the pitfalls of the heretics dwindles almost to insignificance relative to these considerations. It is for freedom that Christ has set us free, and that freedom is not only a freedom *from* error, but much more importantly, a freedom *for* worship, a freedom for faith and hope and love.

Orthodoxy, then, can be too narrowly conceived as a negative condition: hence the turn to Biblical Trinitarianism in the preceding chapter. But that chapter itself tackled another danger associated with being orthodox: *improperly constructed* orthodoxy. Hyper-orthodoxy, the desire to defend orthodox belief by any means (even by interpolating additional texts, such as the Johannine Comma, into Scripture) is one such way in which orthodoxy can be wrongly established. There are others, and in this Epilogue, I want to delve further into the dangers associated with *orthodox*, rather than just heretical, belief.

There is the danger that is twinned with hyper-orthodoxy, its equal and opposite error: hypo-orthodoxy, the belief that orthodoxy is inherently dangerous and should therefore be reduced to the lowest possible level. The two errors tend to feed off each other. As the hyper-orthodox feel that right belief is under threat from liberalizers and minimalists, so the hypo-orthodox feel that right belief is at risk from fundamentalists, rigorists and conservatives.

Hypo-orthodoxy is a common and entirely understandable reaction to religious fanaticism. If one has been brought up in a suffocatingly religious household or educated in a militantly religious school, it will be natural, once one has worked free of it, to think, 'Never again! No such extremism for me. These hard-and-fast truth-claims are not the essence of orthodoxy; I will give them a wide berth from now on.' But orthodoxy which is defined by its reaction against something heterodox (wrong) or unorthodox (not necessarily wrong, but eccentric) is precariously founded. The opposite of extremism is not necessarily balance and tolerance; it might just as well be an alternative kind of extremism. To say that all truth-claims are dangerous is itself a truth-claim, a liberal truth-claim that has handily been exchanged for the old conservative one. In a quasi-Gnostic fashion, the hypo-orthodox have a vague idea of a *pleroma* – a sense of fullness, or oneness, a vision of everyone getting along with everyone else – and, again rather like the Gnostics, the hypo-orthodox possess a secret knowledge or wisdom which gives access to this ideal state. Their gnosis can be summed up in the line: 'Compassion and acceptance are the essence of right belief.' In an attempt to avoid hyper-orthodox rigidity and judge-mentalism, they overbalance; they overlook the 'hard sayings' of Jesus about cutting off hands and plucking out eyes, putting millstones round necks, and treating an unrepentant brother like a Gentile or tax-collector. They fail to hold these things in proper tension with his teachings about forgiveness, forbearance and inclusivity.

Is orthodoxy then to be defined as a kind of balance, a mid-point between the hyper and the hypo? Such a definition has a good deal going for it. Don't just accelerate into frantic hyper-orthodoxy; use the brake too. Don't just sputter into hypo-orthodoxy; keep the engine turning. We have found this need for balance throughout our investigations in this book: Jesus divine, but also human; Jesus human, but also divine; his natures inseparable, but also unconfused; his natures unchanged, but also indivisible; his root in the Old Testament, but also his flower and fruit in the New; the call for Levitical purity, but also Levitical generosity; the need not only to limit and describe, but also to say more and more. A 'both/and'

approach, it seems, is nearly always required in order to appre-
hend the truth, a willingness to meet half-way: 'moderation in
all things'.

As a native member of the Church of England, I am perhaps
too ready to extol this 'both/and' approach; the famous British
compromise and the Anglican *via media* are bred in the bone.
But having the best of both worlds is often also a good and
biblical way of thinking Christianly. I must have not only faith,
but also works (James 2.24). I must be a citizen of both earth
and heaven (Matthew 22.21). I must be as cunning as a serpent
and as innocent as a dove (Matthew 10.16). And so on. We
may usefully think of orthodoxy as doctrinal equanimity, and
both in negative and positive modes. Orthodoxy is the ability
to resist errors from the right and errors from the left with equal
vigour, and the ability to embrace truths from the right and
truths from the left with equal fervour. The result is the capacity to walk straight, which is a very common Old Testament
image of righteousness: 'I will turn aside neither to the right
hand nor to the left' (Deuteronomy 2.27; 5.32; 28.14; Joshua
1.7; 23.6; Proverbs 4.27).

But this balanced 'both/and' mindset must itself be internally
balanced: what we require is *both* 'both/and' *and* 'either/or'.
Moderation in all things, including moderation! If we think that
balance is the be-all and end-all we will be selling orthodoxy
short, for there is such a thing as excessive balance; and this
is the third danger associated with orthodoxy that we have to
consider. It comes in two forms. One form is lukewarmness.
Orthodox balance consists in more than coolly splitting the difference between pairs of errors; it is more than the combining
of polar truths into a neutral middle-ground. Falling between
two stools may be worse than either of the extremisms we have
already mentioned. Hyper-orthodoxy and hypo-orthodoxy at
least leave their adherents looking like human beings, however
rabid or complacent. But this unnatural symmetry, this calcu-
lated colonization of the dead-point between two transmitters,

this insistent compromise, is robotic. It is no surprise that lukewarmness is a scriptural image of evil (Revelation 3.15–16), nor that the first commandment is to love God with *all* our heart, soul, mind and strength: no qualification or reservation. Either we aim for that goal or we don't; there are to be no half-measures. Let the orthodox become passionately conservative or passionately liberal before they become unimpassioned and indifferent like this. Orthodoxy is a matter of the heart and soul, not just of balance.

And the second way in which balance can become excessive is in the attitude Christians adopt to those outside the Church. Christianity is not a dualistic faith. Acceptance of orthodoxy (in all its doctrinal balance) ought not to involve the corollary of an equal and opposite rejection of heterodoxy – because the two things are not equal and opposite. The opposite of the devil is not God, but the archangel Michael. God has no opposite and the creeds – it may be worth pointing out – do not require any kind of belief in Satan. It is impossible to reject error with the same resolution with which one embraces truth for the simple reason that error does not have the same reality as truth. The orthodox need to remember this, especially if they feel themselves to be on the back foot, when the temptation to 'give as good as you get' becomes strong. By remembering that orthodoxy denies dualism, we will be helped to preserve a due sense of proportion about heterodoxy – and especially about those we consider to be heterodox.

This book is called *Heresies and How to Avoid Them*, not *Heretics and How to Avoid Them*. Our purpose has not been to outline principles for church governance and discipline (though we may perhaps mention certain key texts pertinent to a scriptural discussion of the issue, such as Matthew 18.15–18; Romans 14.1–23; 1 Corinthians 6.1–8; 2 Corinthians 6.14–18; 2 Thessalonians 3.6, 14–15). We have simply been concerned to point out that membership of the Christian Church has always been understood as being equally open to all: men and women, rich and poor, Jew and Gentile, young and old. By one Spirit we were all baptized into one body. Membership is defined by what we believe and do and say, not by what we are or who we are according to sexual or social or racial categorizations. Obviously, the Church must set limits on what we may believe and do and say or else the title 'Christian' becomes synonymous with 'anyone who happens to want that title', which would be effectively meaningless. This book has shown that the Church has always been inclusive of all ontologies and always exclusive of certain beliefs and behaviours, but it is not in our remit to pursue the question, 'How should the Church act with respect to those who propagate heresy?' For further discussion of the subject we must point the reader elsewhere: Michael Thompson's little book *When Should We Divide? Schism and Discipline in the New Testament* might be a good place to start.

The necessary exclusivity of church membership may come to be seen as the defining feature of orthodoxy: this is the next danger that we have to consider. The orthodox may be tempted to think that their chief duty is to exclude the heterodox. Exclusion may eventually seem insufficient; perhaps extermination would be safer. Soon Christians will be torturing and killing in the name of orthodoxy. The notion that the category of orthodoxy leads only to the stake, the block, and the burning of books lies behind much of the contemporary mistrust of religion, the Christian Church not excepted. Unfortunately, it is true that Christianity has led to all those things. Orthodoxy can be turned into a weapon against the heterodox, an excuse for any and every kind of outrage. But does the category of orthodoxy only and always land us in that shambles? Logically and historically: no. It has not always led even to excommunication, and if we examine the Church's record in dealing with the heretics mentioned in this book we will see that the popular picture of fire-breathing prelates is actually far from accurate. Arius was banished, but recalled, and Athanasius was ordered to receive him back into communion. Apollinarius lived to a ripe old age and himself seceded from the Church. After Nestorius's views were condemned, he was sent back to his monastery at Antioch, though he was eventually exiled to Upper Egypt. Eutyches was also deposed and exiled. Elipandus (of the Adoptionists) retained possession of his bishopric all his life, and Peter the Fuller (of the Theopaschites) was still patriarch of Antioch at the time of his death. Marcion, like Pelagius, was excommunicated. Valentinus (the Gnostic) seceded. None of these men had his blood shed on account of his views. I trust I am not so naive as to assume that killing or physically wounding someone is always the worst thing you can do to them – there is more than one way to skin a heretic – but let it at least be stated that none of these men died or bled when his opinions were denounced. It is a prejudice to assume that heresy-hunters are all torturers and sadists or in hock to the same: history doesn't support it.

Of the heresies discussed in this book, two occasioned bloodshed. The Donatists were violently suppressed by their fellow Christians. If it is any exculpation (which it may well not be), it should be remembered that these acts of suppression were carried out in retaliation for attacks committed by the Donatists themselves, and that this whole controversy was itself born out of the Roman Emperor Diocletian's persecution of the Church. It should also be borne in mind that the Donatists were not eliminated. Far from it; they continued to exist alongside orthodox communities for three and a half centuries.

Only one of the heretics whom we have discussed paid the ultimate price: Marguerite Porete. That is one too many, but we should give due weight to the fact that her fate is the exception, not the rule. Also, we should note that the 'heresy of the Free Spirit' comes substantially later than any of the other heresies discussed in these pages, in the fourteenth century. The Church of the Middle Ages forsook the pacific approach which very largely characterized the Church during the first millennium of its history, and there was much bloodshed during the Inquisition and the Reformation (to use two large and crude labels). In general, it is no more true that 'orthodoxy always causes violence' than it is true that 'race' or 'politics' or 'money' or any other huge generalization leads to any one thing. With respect to the major controversies of the first thousand years of the Church, we can say that, almost invariably, disagreements over heresies were settled in a non-violent way. We could learn something from that period of history if we paid more attention to it.

But even if orthodox church membership does not lead to violence, it may lead to other serious mistakes. One is hypocrisy. Since believing and saying and doing the things that will get us recognized as orthodox are functions or practices, they can easily be aped. Orthodoxy is imitable. In a religion with an ontologically defined membership this would be less of a problem: a woman can't easily pretend to be a man; a poor person can't easily pretend to be rich. But in the Christian Church, with its membership defined by beliefs and behaviours, pretence is a recurrent and debilitating infection. Tennyson's famous line from *In Memoriam*, 'There lives more faith in honest doubt, believe me, than in half the creeds' (where 'creeds' means 'those who *say* they subscribe to the creeds'), is a just rebuke of the dishonesty which can batten on the back of sincerity.

But there is something worse than the hypocrisy to which orthodoxy is susceptible: it is the idolatry. As soon as creeds have been accepted, orthodox behaviour appears to demand assent to them rather than to the God to whom they point. Thus the opportunity for new error is born even in the act of distinguishing truth: we may ascribe ultimate value to our creedal formulations, as if they were the end of spiritual life, rather than the banister by which we are helped to climb to that end. But creeds are only a brief summary of the scriptures, which are themselves only a means to Christ, not an end, as Jesus told the religious leaders of his day: 'You search the scriptures, because you think that in them you have eternal life; and it is they that bear witness to me; yet you refuse to come to me that you may have life' (John 5.39). We must not make our spoon into our meat.

While Moses was caught up by that spiritual thunderstorm in which his reception of the ten commandments was forged (Exodus 19.16–25), simultaneously his fellow Israelites were making the golden calf (Exodus 32.1–6). We may interpret these events allegorically: closer knowledge of God allows more abominable betrayal, or 'new doughnuts make new holes'. Every time the people of God are led into truth, the advance is accompanied by fresh risk.

In addition to the six corruptions of orthodoxy which we have so far considered (negatively defined orthodoxy; the two-headed monster of hyper- and hypo-orthodoxy; excessive balance; violence; hypocrisy; idolatry), there is one last danger to examine, making a very imperfect seven in total. It came close to being mentioned in the opening chapter when Michael Thompson pointed out that what separated the supporters of Arius from the supporters of Athanasius could be summarized by a single Greek letter. Between *homoousios* and *homoiousios* there is only an iota's difference (p. 19). Is this worth bothering with? Does it really matter? Is orthodoxy not just a vast pedantry? In the case of Arianism, the iota did in fact make all the difference in the world, but is that always the case with the fine discriminations that cluster about Christian doctrine? Cannot credal precision be sometimes pressed too far? This is the final danger we have to consider: the danger of orthodoxy turning into barren intellectualism, something to entertain academics and theologians, but without any purchase upon actual daily life.

The way to avoid this danger is to remember the motto 'No creeds without deeds': in other words, orthodoxy mustn't be separated from orthopraxy – right belief is inextricably linked with right practice. Jeremy Taylor, a seventeenth-century

Anglican theologian, once wrote that 'heresy is not an error of the understanding but an error of the will', and the poet Coleridge, commenting upon this remark, added, 'Most excellent. To this Taylor should have adhered, and to its converse: Faith is not an accuracy of logic but a rectitude of the heart.' Orthodoxy is of course a matter of the intellect, but not only of the intellect; it is also a matter of the will and the heart and the soul and the body – the whole person living out the truth of the gospel daily in thought, feeling, spirituality and action. As John the evangelist reminds us, if we would know and understand Christian doctrine, we must actually *do* God's will (John 7.17).

This book has limited itself mostly to discussing orthodoxy from an intellectual perspective. The limitation has been deliberate, but it will also have been disastrous if it leaves the impression that we can grasp orthodoxy exclusively with our minds. Orthodoxy is far too rich, subtle, lively and paradoxical to be reduced to a set of philosophical categories. We must never presume to think that we can suck the heart out of its mystery. To construe it as something apprehensible by the intellect alone would be to suggest that what we're talking about is merely a proposition, something lying inert and analysable in a system of thought. But in reality, Christian orthodoxy, understood properly, is not something that we can fully grasp, still less dissect. Rather, it is a means of keeping ourselves exposed to the truth which grasps us. And what is the nature of that truth?

One cannot frame such a question without Francis Bacon's famous line coming immediately to mind: '"What is truth?" asked jesting Pilate and would not stay for an answer.' Pilate's error lay not only in not staying for an answer, it lay also in the formulation of his question: '*What* is truth?' as if truth were merely a thing or an idea or a concept. Moreover, Pilate asked it (with awful and unintended irony) of the one who had said, '*I* am the truth.' The answer was standing there in front of him.

Truth, first and foremost, is not an 'it', not a proposition, but a person, who will always elude over-precise descriptions. Jesus Christ is the one with whom we have to do. We avoid heresies and we avoid the dangers associated with orthodoxy because we have encountered him in his Spirit and because we hope to encounter him one day face to face in the kingdom of his Father.

Glossary

———◆•◆———

Adoptionism See p. 50.

antinomian Literally, 'against law'. Paul was accused of antinomianism by his opponents (Romans 3.8) because they thought he disparaged the Mosaic Law in favour of the New Covenant 'written on the heart', a charge he repudiated.

Apollinarianism (a kind of Docetism) See p. 24.

Arianism See p. 15.

begotten Generated, produced out of oneself, as distinct from being made out of something other than oneself; e.g. birds *beget* birds, but *make* nests. To say of Jesus Christ that he is eternally begotten by God the Father, not made by him, is to say that he shares the very nature of God the Father.

canonical Belonging to the canon of officially approved Scripture; among the writings held by the Church to possess apostolic authority.

catholic Of or relating to the universal Christian Church; distinct from 'Roman Catholic'.

Chalcedonian Of or relating to the Council of Chalcedon, held in the year 451.

Christology The doctrine or study of the person and teachings of Christ.

circumcelliones In the Donatist controversy, those who deliberately sought a martyr's death as a means of grace, sometimes provoking their own death through violent behaviour.

conciliar Of or relating to a general, ecumenical Council of the Church.

cosmogony A theory or account of the origin of the universe.

creed A statement of faith; examples of official, Church-sanctioned creeds include the Apostles' Creed and the Nicene Creed (see pp. 10–11).

demiurge Literally, 'public maker', a deity or creative force (e.g. in Gnostic thought) who makes the material world and is often viewed as the originator of evil.

Docetism See p. 24.

doctrine A teaching, a formulation of theological thought expressing religious belief.

Donatism See p. 81.

doxology An expression of praise to God, especially a short hymn sung as part of a public service of worship.

dualism Belief in a permanent or essential duality, with respect to e.g. good and evil, divinity and humanity, matter and spirit, masculinity and femininity.

ecumenical Of or relating to the catholic Church (from Greek *oikos*, meaning 'house, household').

Eucharist Literally, 'thanksgiving'; another term for Holy Communion or the Lord's Supper.

Eutychianism See p. 41.

'Free Spirit' See p. 113.

gnosis Literally, 'knowledge'; a special, non-rational apprehension of spiritual truths, an esoteric form of wisdom.

Gnosticism See p. 102.

heresy A doctrine believed or taught in opposition to the conciliar definitions of the undivided, catholic Church.

heretic A baptized person who obstinately denies or doubts a truth which the Church teaches must be believed because it is part of the one, catholic, and divinely revealed Christian faith.

heterodox Other than that which is orthodox, opposed to or incompatible with orthodoxy.

homoousios Of the same substance or essence; orthodox term used to describe the relationship between the three persons of the Trinity, and especially between Christ and God the Father.

homoiousios Of similar substance or essence; heterodox description of the relationship between Christ and God the Father.

hypostasis Basis, foundation, underlying reality, inner nature beneath the outer form, individual principle of being; closely related to *ousia*.

impassible Not naturally subject to suffering.

incarnate Made human, enfleshed.

Johannine Comma A comma or short clause concerning the doctrine of the Trinity found in most translations of the First Epistle of John published between 1522 and the second half of the nineteenth century.

liturgical Of or relating to liturgy, the form of public ceremony or ritual used in religious worship.

logos A term from Greek philosophy used to describe the inherent order of the universe, its underlying rationality and meaningfulness; later used in the prologue of John's Gospel to describe Jesus Christ and usually translated into English as 'Word': 'In the beginning was the Word, and the Word was with God, and the Word was God ... And the Word became flesh and dwelt among us' (John 1.1, 14).

Marcionism See p. 73.

Miaphysite The belief that Christ has one nature, but that that nature is *of the two natures*, divine and human; the Christology of the Oriental Orthodox Churches. It has often been regarded by Western Churches as Monophysite, but the Oriental Orthodox Churches themselves reject this.

Monophysite The heretical belief that Christ has only one nature, as opposed to the orthodox Chalcedonian position which states that Christ has two natures in one person. The most extreme form of Monophysitism is Eutychianism.

Nestorianism See p. 32.

ontology The study of being or existence.

orthodoxy Right belief, correct doctrine, as determined by the Ecumenical Councils of the Church.

orthopraxy Right practice, behaviour consistent with orthodoxy.

ousia Essence or substance, a form of the Greek verb 'to be'; closely related to *hypostasis*.

Pelagianism See p. 91.

pleroma In Gnostic thought, the fullness of God's powers, the Light existing above our world, the totality of the divine emanations.

schism Formal and wilful separation from the unity of the Church; distinct from heresy in that the separation involved is not essentially doctrinal. Schism opposes charity; heresy opposes faith.

Shekinah The radiance of the divine presence, the manifest glory of God's indwelling.

Stoic Of or relating to the ancient Greek school of philosophy, founded by Zeno, which taught that virtue consisted in submission to destiny and in indifference to pleasure or pain.

Theopaschitism See p. 59.

theophages Literally, 'God-eaters'. In pagan religion, worshippers would consume a sacred food (e.g. a sacrificed animal, or grain, or an aphrodisiac) in order to secure blessing from and identity with the deity to whom it was symbolically related; sometimes used, usually pejoratively, of the Eucharist.

theophany A manifestation or appearance of God to man.

theotokos Literally, 'God-bearer'; a title of the Virgin Mary, denoting her as the mother of God.

traditores Literally, 'those who hand over'; used of those Christians who, under persecution by the Emperor Diocletian, handed over church vessels and sacred books, and betrayed their fellow Christians.

Trinity The threefold nature of the Christian God: one God in three persons (or one *ousia* in three *hypostases*), the Father, the Son, and the Holy Spirit.

unorthodox Irregular, independent, breaking with convention or tradition; possibly, but not necessarily, heterodox.

For further reading

C. Fitzsimmons Allison, *The Cruelty of Heresy: An Affirmation of Christian Orthodoxy* (SPCK, 1994).

Henry Chadwick, *Heresy and Orthodoxy in the Early Church* (Variorum, 1991).

F. L. Cross and E. A. Livingstone (eds), *The Oxford Dictionary of the Christian Church* (Oxford University Press, 1997).

Stuart G. Hall, *Doctrine and Practice in the Early Church* (SPCK, 1991).

St Irenaeus, Bishop of Lyons, *Against the Heresies*, translated and annotated by Dominic J. Unger, with further revisions by John J. Dillon (Paulist Press, 1992).

Joan O'Grady, *Heresy: Heretical Truth or Orthodox Error?* (Element Books, 1985).

Dorothy L. Sayers, *Creed or Chaos?* (Hodder & Stoughton, 1940).

J. Stevenson (ed.), *Creeds, Councils and Controversies: Documents Illustrating the History of the Church A.D. 337–461* (SPCK, 1989).

Michael B. Thompson, *When Should We Divide? Schism and Discipline in the New Testament* (Grove Books, 2004).

Frances M. Young, *The Making of the Creeds* (SCM Press, 2002).

Biblical references index

Genesis
1.9 76
1.26–27 24–5, 29
1.31 102
1—2 107, 108

Exodus
3.1–15 130
19.16–25 139
20.18–21 73, 75
32.1–6 139

Leviticus
11.44 86
19.1–2 82
19.11–12 82
19.17–19 82
19.19 87
19.33–37 82

Numbers
21.8 76
23.19 63

Deuteronomy
2.27 134
5.32 134
28.14 134

Joshua
1.7 134
23.6 134

2 Samuel
5—24 76

1 Kings
19.8–13 130

2 Kings
5.1–5 91–2
5.9–14 91–2

Psalms
8 28, 38
14 98
14.1–3 97
14.7 97
85 39

Proverbs
4.27 134
8 110

Isaiah
6.3 40
42.8 22
45.5 22
45.6 22
45.14 22
45.18 22
45.21 22
45.22 22
45.22–23 21
49.1–7 50–1, 56

Malachi
3.6 59, 63

Wisdom
1.12–15 33

Matthew
5.17–20 74, 76
5.48 113, 114, 115, 119
10.16 134
13.24–30 82–3, 87–8
13.30 87
18.15–18 135
19.17 17
22.21 134
25.40 30
25.45 30
28.19 122

Mark
13.32 27
14.36 28
15.34 28

Luke
1.38 39
3.15–17 51
3.21–22 51
3.22 55, 122, 129
9.28–36 122, 123, 129
9.35 129
22.42 18

John
1.1 18, 21, 22, 144
1.1–14 32–3, 38
1.14 21, 38, 108, 122, 130, 144
1.18 21
4.3–10 41–2
5.18 29
5.19–20 29
5.39 138–9
7.17 140
8.58 27
10.10 132
14.6 140
14.12 30
14.28 18
19.1–11a 59–60
19.11 69
20.19b–29 16, 22
20.28 22
20.31 129

Romans
3 98
3.8 142
3.9–12 93, 94
3.19–28 93, 94
3.23 96
5 39
8.21 58
8.29 31
9.5 21
14.1–23 135

1 Corinthians
6.1–8 135
8.6 21
11.19 42
13 9

2 Corinthians
4.6 128
6.14–18 135
8.9 21

Galatians
2.20b 114, 120
4.1–7 33, 39
4.4 21

Ephesians
5.14 26

Philippians
2 21
2.5–11 15–16
2.6 21, 54
2.9–11 21

Colossians
1.15–20 21
2.9 21

2 Thessalonians
3.6 135
3.14–15 135

1 Timothy
6.20–21 103

2 Timothy
2.13 63, 66

Titus
2.13 21

Hebrews
4.14–16 42
5.7–9 25, 26
5.8 29
13.8 63

James
1.17 63
2.24 134

2 Peter
3.14 86

1 John
3.2 29
4 65
5.5–9 (KJV) 122, 123
5.7 (KJV) 125
5.7–9 (KJV) 124
5.9 126
5.13 128, 129

Revelation
3.15–16 135

General index

Abraham 27
Adam 40, 76, 96, 100
Adams, Nicholas xi, 91
Adoptionism 4, 26, **50–8**,
  61, 137, 142
Against Heresies see Irenaeus
  of Lyons
Alexander, Bishop of
  Alexandria 19
Allison, C. Fitzsimmons 131,
  146; *The Cruelty of Heresy*
  131, 146
Anglicanism 6, 134, 140
Anselm of Canterbury 63
anti-Semitism 80, 131
apatheia 66
Apollinarianism 4, 24, 32,
  34, 45, 113, 142
Apollinarius of Laodicea 24,
  27, 30, 44, 137
Apostles' Creed 10, 128, 142
Aquinas, Thomas 63
Arianism 3–4, **15–23**, 25, 34,
  60, 67, 122, 127, 139, 142
Aristotle 61
Arius 15, 17–20, 22, 27, 93,
  136, 139
Arles, Synod of 81
Athanasian Creed 69
Athanasius 15, 19, 27, 44,
  105, 109, 136, 139
Auden, W. H. 67
Augustine of Hippo 81, 84,
  86–8, 90–1, 94, 96–8,
  100
Auschwitz 63

Bacon, Sir Francis 140
baptism 11, 26, 39, 51–3, 57,
  86–7, 89–90, 129, 136,
  143
Basilides 102
Begbie, Jeremy 8; *Sounding
  the Depths: Theology
  Through the Arts* 8
Benedict of Nursia 101
Bergquist, Anders xi, 102

Blake, William 29
Bonhoeffer, Dietrich 90;
  Ethics 90
Book of Common Prayer 10,
  11, 89–90
Brown, Dan 109; *The Da
  Vinci Code* 109–10

Caecilian 81
Calvin, John 124–5
Cambridge, University of
  xi–xiv, 124, 127
Chadwick, Henry 84–5, 87,
  89, 146; *Augustine* 84–5,
  87, 89, 146
Chalcedon, Council of 4, 12,
  41, 45, 67, 142
Chalcedonian Definition 12,
  46, 60
Chesterton, G. K. 60;
  Orthodoxy 60
circumcelliones 86, 142
Clement of Alexandria 73,
  104
Coleridge, Samuel Taylor
  140
Constantine the Great,
  Emperor 85
Constantinople, Council of
  4, 11, 19, 24
Copernicus, Nicolaus 63
Cyril, patriarch of Alexandria
  32, 44–6

David, King 76
demiurge 18–19, 23, 102,
  106–7, 142
Diocletian, Emperor 81, 84,
  137, 144
Docetism **24–31**, 34, 60, 65,
  69, 79, 127, 142–3
Docetists 4, 24, 67
Donatism **81–90**, 113, 121,
  137, 142–3
Donatus, bishop of Carthage
  81, 85
Durkheim, Emile 127

Eckhart, Meister 119
Elijah 123, 129
Eliot, George 127
Elipandus, archbishop of
  Toledo 50, 52–4, 137
Elisha 91–2
Ephesus, Council of 4, 32, 44
Erasmus, Desiderius 124–5
Escrivá de Balaguer,
  Josemaría 114
Eucharist 45, 47, 86–7, 89,
  95, 101, 137, 143, 145
Eutyches 4, 41, 43–7, 137
Eutychianism 4, 34, **41–9**,
  60–1, 143–4
Eve 40
excommunication 89, 95,
  136–7

Felix of Aptunga 81
Frankfurt, Council of 50
Free Spirit, heresy of **113–21**,
  137, 143
Freud, Sigmund 127

gnosis 25, 102–3, 133, 143
Gnosticism 25, 62, **102–12**,
  142–4
Gnostics 24, 26, 133, 137

Hadrian I, Pope 50, 52
Harnack, Adolf von 77,
  79–80
Helen of Troy 25
Herakleon 107
heresies: ambiguous 114;
  a category imposed by
  opponents 43; compiled to
  match their condemnation
  116; as danger areas 31;
  defined 1, 42, 60, 143;
  degree of truth in 25;
  detection of somewhat
  artificial 43; disagreements
  over settled non-violently
  138; an essential concept
  43; a good thing 42;